Understanding
World History

Victorian
England

Other titles in the series include:

Ancient Egypt
Ancient Greece
Ancient Rome
The Black Death
The Decade of the 2000s
The Digital Age
The Early Middle Ages
Elizabethan England
The Great Recession
The History of Rock and Roll
The Holocaust
The Industrial Revolution
The Late Middle Ages
Pearl Harbor
The Renaissance

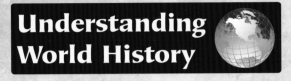

Understanding World History

Victorian England

Gail B. Stewart

Bruno Leone
Series Consultant

ReferencePoint Press®

San Diego, CA

© 2014 ReferencePoint Press, Inc.
Printed in the United States

For more information, contact:
ReferencePoint Press, Inc.
PO Box 27779
San Diego, CA 92198
www.ReferencePointPress.com

LIBRARY OF CONGRESS CATALOGING-IN-PUBLICATION DATA

Stewart, Gail B. (Gail Barbara), 1949–
  Victorian England / by Gail B. Stewart.
    pages cm. -- (Understanding world history series)
  Includes bibliographical references and index.
  ISBN-13: 978-1-60152-602-1 (hardback) -- ISBN-10: 1-60152-602-4 (hardback) 1. Great Britain--History--Victoria, 1837-1901. 2. Great Britain--Social conditions--19th century. 3. Great Britain--Social life and customs--19th century. 4. Great Britain--Civilization--19th century. I. Title.
  DA550.S738   2013
  942.081--dc23
                                            2013018908

Contents

When the Puritans first emigrated from England to America in 1630, they believed that their journey was blessed by a covenant between themselves and God. By the terms of that covenant they agreed to establish a community in the New World dedicated to what they believed was the true Christian faith. God, in turn, would reward their fidelity by making certain that they and their descendants would always experience his protection and enjoy material prosperity. Moreover, the Lord guaranteed that their land would be seen as a shining beacon—or in their words, a "city upon a hill,"—which the rest of the world would view with admiration and respect. By embracing this notion that God could and would shower his favor and special blessings upon them, the Puritans were adopting the providential philosophy of history—meaning that history is the unfolding of a plan established or guided by a higher intelligence.

The concept of intercession by a divine power is only one of many explanations of the driving forces of world history. Historians and philosophers alike have subscribed to numerous other ideas. For example, the ancient Greeks and Romans argued that history is cyclical. Nations and civilizations, according to these ancients of the Western world, rise and fall in unpredictable cycles; the only certainty is that these cycles will persist throughout an endless future. The German historian Oswald Spengler (1880–1936) echoed the ancients to some degree in his controversial study *The Decline of the West*. Spengler asserted that all civilizations inevitably pass through stages comparable to the life span of a person: childhood, youth, adulthood, old age, and, eventually, death. As the title of his work implies, Western civilization is currently entering its final stage.

Joining those who see purpose and direction in history are thinkers who completely reject the idea of meaning or certainty. Rather, they reason that since there are far too many random and unseen factors at work on the earth, historians would be unwise to endorse historical predictability of any type. Warfare (both nuclear and conventional), plagues, earthquakes, tsunamis, meteor showers, and other catastrophic world-changing events have loomed large throughout history and prehistory. In his essay "A Free Man's Worship," philosopher and mathematician Bertrand Russell (1872–1970) supported this argument, which many refer to as the nihilist or chaos theory of history. According to Russell, history follows no preordained path. Rather, the earth itself and all life on earth resulted from, as Russell describes it, an "accidental collocation of atoms." Based on this premise, he pessimistically concluded that all human achievement will eventually be "buried beneath the debris of a universe in ruins."

Whether history does or does not have an underlying purpose, historians, journalists, and countless others have nonetheless left behind a record of human activity tracing back nearly 6,000 years. From the dawn of the great ancient Near Eastern civilizations of Mesopotamia and Egypt to the modern economic and military behemoths China and the United States, humanity's deeds and misdeeds have been and continue to be monitored and recorded. The distinguished British scholar Arnold Toynbee (1889–1975), in his widely acclaimed twelve-volume work entitled *A Study of History*, studied twenty-one different civilizations that have passed through history's pages. He noted with certainty that others would follow.

In the final analysis, the academic and journalistic worlds mostly regard history as a record and explanation of past events. From a more practical perspective, history represents a sequence of building blocks—cultural, technological, military, and political—ready to be utilized and enhanced or maligned and perverted by the present. What that means is that all societies—whether advanced civilizations or preliterate tribal cultures—leave a legacy for succeeding generations to either embrace or disregard.

Recognizing the richness and fullness of history, the ReferencePoint Press Understanding World History series fosters an evaluation and interpretation of history and its influence on later generations. Each volume in the series approaches its subject chronologically and topically, with specific focus on nations, periods, or pivotal events. Primary and secondary source quotations are included, along with complete source notes and suggestions for further research.

Moreover, the series reflects the truism that the key to understanding the present frequently lies in the past. With that in mind, each series title concludes with a legacy chapter that highlights the bonds between past and present and, more important, demonstrates that world history is a continuum of peoples and ideas, sometimes hidden but there nonetheless, waiting to be discovered by those who choose to look.

Important Events in the Era of Victorian England

1789
The French Revolution begins, eventually resulting in the execution of King Louis XVI and his wife, Marie Antoinette, horrifying the aristocracy in Britain.

1843
The first Christmas cards are sent, the idea of entrepreneur Sir Henry Cole, who is too busy to write individual letters wishing his many friends a happy holiday, as he has always done in the past.

1769
Scottish inventor James Watt improves the steam engine, making it smaller and more reliable.

1838
Charles Dickens's novel *Oliver Twist* is published, calling attention to the deplorable conditions in workhouses.

1750   **1800**   **1850**

1815
The British defeat Napoleon at Waterloo, Belgium, on June 18, effectively ending the Napoleonic Wars. Waterloo Day becomes an annual national holiday in Britain.

1830
England's first passenger railroad line, the Liverpool and Manchester Railway, opens with a ribbon-cutting ceremony.

1819
Victoria is born in England on May 24 to Prince Edward, the fourth son of George III, and Victoria, a princess of a region in what is now Germany.

1845
The Irish potato famine begins as farmers throughout the country discover their entire potato crop is wiped out. The famine lasts six years and results in the deaths of more than 1 million people.

1851
The Great Exhibition, largely the creation of Prince Albert, opens in Hyde Park, London, with more than one hundred thousand exhibits from all over the world.

1856
Victoria initiates the Victoria Cross, the nation's highest honor for military courage. The metal that the first medals are made of is from melted-down Russian cannons captured during the Crimean War.

1901
Victoria dies, and her son Albert Edward becomes King Edward VII.

1873
Explorer and missionary David Livingstone dies in an African country now known as Zambia.

1897
Britain celebrates Victoria's Diamond Jubilee (sixty years on the throne).

1850   **1875**   **1900**

1861
Albert dies of typhoid fever. A heartbroken Victoria begins wearing black mourning clothes and continues to wear black until her death forty years later.

1859
Naturalist Charles Darwin publishes *On the Origin of Species*, causing outrage among many who feel he is contradicting the biblical version of Creation.

1857
The Indian Mutiny breaks out after Indian troops refuse to fire their rifles containing controversial cartridges.

1854
Reporter William Howard Russell files his first story from the front of the Crimean War for the *Times*, a London newspaper; motivated by reading Russell's stories, Florence Nightingale travels to the Crimea to provide medical support to British troops suffering from disease and battle wounds.

What Were the Defining Characteristics of Victorian England?

On June 20, 1837, just before dawn, eighteen-year-old Princess Victoria was awakened by her mother. The archbishop of Canterbury and the lord chamberlain (a chief officer of the royal household in Britain) were waiting to see Victoria with important news. After pulling on her robe, Victoria hurried into the drawing room where the visitors were waiting.

They had two important announcements to relay. The first was that her uncle, King William IV, had died during the night. She immediately knew what the second announcement was without being told. As the two men knelt in front of her, she knew that she was no longer Princess Victoria. Overnight, she had become Queen Victoria, reigning monarch of the British Empire.

An Unlikely Queen

When Victoria was born on May 24, 1819, no one would have predicted that she would ever become queen. Her grandfather, King George III, had fifteen children, of whom Victoria's father, Edward, was fifth in the line of succession. It seemed almost certain that one of George's elder sons or his daughter Charlotte would rule and have children who would eventually inherit the throne.

But that did not happen. Two of George's children, Frederick and Charlotte, died. After the death of King George III in 1820, his eldest son became King George IV, ruling until his death in 1830. He had no

Queen Victoria became England's monarch at age eighteen. She ruled England during a time of rapid social, economic, and political change.

legitimate children. (Children conceived outside of marriage were not eligible for succession to the throne.) William IV, the next eldest son of George III, was next in line. He ruled for only seven years before his death in 1837. The next eldest son, Edward, had died years before. As a result, Edward's daughter Victoria became heir to the throne.

The idea of a teenage girl ruling one of the world's most powerful nations must have been startling to many of Victoria's subjects, who probably wondered how someone so young could handle the thorny issues of the huge British Empire. As he watched the coronation procession, Thomas Carlyle, a Scottish writer and historian popular in nineteenth-century Britain, wrote, "Poor little queen; she is at an age at which a girl can hardly be trusted to choose a bonnet for herself; yet a task is laid upon her from which an archangel might shrink."[1]

However, the new queen herself seemed to have had no misgivings about her youth or her ability to take on the nation's most difficult problems. In her journal entry for Tuesday, June 20, 1837, she expresses confidence in her own readiness for the job: "Since it has pleased Providence to place me in this station, I shall do my utmost to fulfill my duty towards my country; I am very young and perhaps in many, though not in all things, inexperienced, but I am sure, that very few have more real good-will and more real desire to do what is fit and right than I have."[2]

Victoria would go on to rule for nearly sixty-four years—longer than any other British monarch. And while there is no doubt that her monarchy was successful in many ways, those successes were not necessarily the result of the queen's actions. Instead, they were due in large part to the rapid changes—social, economic, and political—England was experiencing during her reign.

An Era of Enormous Change

Although the time referred to as the Victorian era often refers to the specific years that Victoria ruled Britain, many historians insist that the Victorian era actually started earlier. Some point to the passage of the Reform Act of 1832 as the start of the era, while others believe that the era began even a bit earlier, in 1824, when the first railroads were built. Whatever the exact year, there is no doubt that Victoria's life coincided with change of all kinds—and at a pace not seen before in history.

According to PBS's *Queen Victoria's Empire*, the world at the time of Victoria's birth "was closer to that of the Greeks and Romans than to the world today."[3] England was largely an agrarian society. In fact, about 95 percent of Britons lived in villages and on farms. The fastest way to travel or send a message was by horseback. The tools people used to do their work by hand—whether farming, sewing, or building—were the same tools their great-grandparents had used, and their great-grandparents before them. In 1819 most people lived their entire lives without traveling more than 10 miles (16 km) from the place they were born.

However, by the time Victoria died in 1901 Britain had become as much an urban nation as a rural one—approximately as many Britons lived in cities as did in small towns and on farms. The population in England had doubled. Transportation had changed, too—the steam locomotive had replaced the horse, making travel faster and easier, with thousands of miles of track linking towns and cities throughout Britain. The nation was also the world's leader in manufacturing, and the British Empire had expanded to include one-quarter of the land and people on Earth.

In June 1897 William Randolph Hearst, the owner of the *San Francisco Examiner*, dispatched American author Mark Twain to London to report on the queen's Diamond Jubilee (sixty years on the throne). Twain, impressed by the ceremony and pageantry of the occasion, became even more so as he realized the sheer magnitude of what had been accomplished in Victoria's reign thus far, writing:

The contrast between the old England and the present England is one of the things that will make the pageant of the present day impressive and thought-breeding. The contrast between the England of the Queen's reign and the England of any previous British reign is also an impressive thing. British history is 2,000 years old, and yet in a good many ways the world has moved further ahead since the Queen was born than in all the rest of the two thousand put together.[4]

Though the amazing transition that Britain went through during Victoria's time was legendary, there were also great difficulties. There was extreme poverty while the wealthy and working classes prospered. The Industrial Revolution brought exciting innovations but also resulted in enormous difficulties in accommodating the ballooning numbers of workers moving to the largest cities in England. And while no wars occurred within Britain itself, the queen's military was not idle during her reign, as upheavals in India and a war in eastern Europe required her to send British soldiers to intercede.

But despite the problems and challenges of the Victorian era, many historians view it as the high point of British civilization. "You think of the Victorians, and you think of a marvelous transition," says Victorian researcher Edward Larsen. "Her reign was a hello to modern life, and goodbye and good riddance to the old ways. And the British seemed as if [they] had found some secret potion in a bottle. The Victorians had such optimism, and pride, and a feeling that [they] should share that bottle with the world, to make everything better."[5]

Chapter 1

What Conditions Led to the Victorian Era?

Though the Victorian era is named for her, Victoria's personal involvement was responsible for only a small fraction of the enormous changes that occurred during her reign. In fact, a great many of those changes occurred because of events that had been set in motion long before her birth.

The Industrial Revolution

Many historians agree that the most important event leading up to the Victorian era was the Industrial Revolution, which began in Britain in the mid-eighteenth century. In a remarkably short period of time, the way in which things were made changed drastically. No longer would people work out of their homes or workshops, sewing or building things either by hand or with the use of simple machines. Instead, they worked in factories using large machines powered by steam.

The steam engine, in fact, started the Industrial Revolution. For years, many had been experimenting with steam with the idea of using its power to run simple machines. In the early 1700s one of the first steam engines was used to run a pump removing water from a coal mine.

However, the pump was immense—the size of a four-story house—and was neither reliable enough nor practical enough for other uses.

In 1769 Scottish inventor James Watt reworked the steam engine to make it more efficient and more reliable. Just as important, Watt's engine could be miniaturized, so it could be used in a variety of machines—large looms in factories, for example, as well as harvesting and threshing machines on farms. Later it was adapted for use in powering locomotives and steamships. There was no doubt that, as PBS notes in its history of the Victorian era, "steam was the genie of the modern age, and it was the British that let it out of the bottle."[6]

The Rise of Coal Production

The Industrial Revolution's effects were more far-reaching than simply the development of new machinery, however. One of the effects of the Industrial Revolution was that coal production had to increase to meet the needs for building and fueling all of those new steam-driven machines.

The immense growth of coal production had a drastic effect on the environment. Coal dust blanketed everything, especially in the English Midlands where most of the nation's coal mines were located. Not surprisingly, this part of England was widely known as "the black country."

Once, when Victoria was thirteen years old, she traveled through the region with her mother and wrote in her journal about how desolate and dark coal production had made it:

We just passed through a town where all coal mines are. . . . The men, women, children, country, and houses are all black. But I cannot by any description give an idea of its strange and extraordinary appearance. The country is very desolate everywhere; there are coals about, and the grass is quite blasted and black. I now see an extraordinary building flaming with fire. The country continues black, engines flaming, coals in abundance, everywhere, smoking and burning coal heaps, intermingled with wretched huts and carts and little ragged children.[7]

Migration to the Cities

Another drastic effect of the Industrial Revolution was the migration of workers from rural areas to cities, including London, Birmingham, Manchester, and Liverpool. With the advent of steam engines powering textile and farm machinery, there were fewer jobs for workers or laborers in workshops and farms. Manufacturing companies were building large factories in cities, where the production of clothing and other goods could take place under one roof.

As a result, more and more people streamed into the cities looking for work in the factories. The flow continued throughout the first half of Victoria's reign: In 1840 just over 75 percent of people lived in small towns and villages. By 1900, at the end of her reign, 75 percent of her

The Industrial Revolution was well under way in England when Victoria rose to the throne. Innovations such as the steam engine advanced both the need for coal and techniques for obtaining and transporting it.

An Assassination Attempt Foiled

Though there was no revolution during her sixty-three-year reign, there were eight attempted assassinations of Queen Victoria. The last occurred On March 2, 1882, when Roderick Maclean fired at the queen as she departed from a railway station in Windsor, on her way to Windsor Castle. The queen was unhurt. Two teenage boys from Eton, who happened to be in the crowd hoping to catch a glimpse of the queen, tackled Maclean and held him until police arrived.

Police learned that Maclean, a poet from Scotland, was angry that the queen had not responded to a poem he had sent to her. At his trial Maclean was found to be insane and was consequently sent to an asylum. The boys who apprehended him, according to a March 4, 1882, edition of the *Manchester Guardian*, were treated like heroes. "It may here be mentioned that two Eton scholars . . . named Wilson and Robinson, who were the means, by hustling the would-be regicide, of saving the life of the Queen, met with a tremendous ovation of applause from their college chums when they returned to Eton last night."

Guardian (Manchester), "From the Archives, March 4, 1882, Victoria Survives Assassination Attempt." www.guardian.co.uk.

subjects were living in large cities. That many people flooding into the cities brought unimaginable problems.

Britain's urban areas were not ready for the massive numbers of people arriving each day. Infrastructures such as water and sewer systems were unable to keep up with the demand, and affordable housing was scarce. The lack of such necessities eventually resulted in an underclass of people who were poor, without adequate housing, and working in low-paying jobs that kept them in impoverished, squalid conditions.

The Locomotive

But while it had negative effects on the cities and the environment, the Industrial Revolution led to inventions that did make life easier for many in Britain. One of the most exciting was the locomotive, invented by George Stephenson in the early 1800s. As far back as 1604, coal miners had transported horse-drawn carts filled with coal from the mines over wooden "wagonways"—tracks made of wooden rails. Stephenson eliminated the need for horses by introducing a modified steam engine that could pull a heavier load than Watts's original engine. His Rocket engine could go at the then unheard-of speed of 24 miles per hour (38.6 kph), and soon chains of carts pulled by locomotive engines were being used to move raw materials and finished goods cheaply and quickly throughout Britain.

Even more fascinating was the notion that people, too, might someday travel on such railways. Frances Ann (Fanny) Kemble, a well-known British actress of the time, writes about her experience of being invited to ride on the inaugural run of Britain's new Liverpool and Manchester line in 1830. Riding on a small, crude train traveling on "two iron bands," as she calls the tracks, was an almost magical experience:

> We were introduced to the little engine which was to drag us along the rails. She . . . consisted of a boiler, a stove, a small platform, a bench, and behind the bench a barrel containing enough water to prevent her from being thirsty for fifteen miles—the whole machine not bigger than a common [horse-drawn] fire engine. . . . You can't imagine how strange it seemed to be journeying on thus, without any visible cause of progress other than the magical machine, with its flying white breath and rhythmical, unvarying pace. . . . I felt as if no fairy tale was ever half so wonderful as what I saw."[8]

Revolution in France

Britons were rightly proud of the technological progress and status they enjoyed because of the Industrial Revolution. However, most had far different feelings about the possibility of another type of revolution—one in which people rose up against their government. Revolution and turmoil within nations was becoming all too common, as British leaders were well aware: During the eighteenth century, Britain's American colonies had revolted against King George III and his taxation policies. The result was a costly war and Britain's disheartening loss of those colonies.

There were other revolutions, too, that were occurring closer to home. For example, Poland had suffered a civil war between 1733 and 1738. In 1830 Belgium fought for independence from Netherlands. There were bloody uprisings in Spain in 1808 and in Portugal in 1820. But it was the revolution in France that most worried the British. They saw France as a nation much like their own, with a monarchy, a strong army, and a vibrant and colorful culture. But in 1789 the impoverished French underclass demanded equality and an end to the inept absolute monarchy of Louis XVI.

Ironically, at first some in England and elsewhere in Europe were impressed by the events unfolding in France. They admired the rebels' desire for freedom and read with interest the reports of their struggle to make France more democratic. But the revolution that began as an attempt by the masses to gain social and political equality was taken over by extremists—and the results were almost too appalling to imagine.

Descent into Terror

The revolution in France deteriorated into a violent, bloody period called the "Reign of Terror." Anyone believed by the extremists to be unsympathetic to their cause could be arrested and then publicly executed by means of the razor-sharp blade of the guillotine. In the eighteen months of the Reign of Terror, more than a thousand people in Paris alone were beheaded. Throughout Europe many—especially wealthy aristocrats—were sickened as they read the news of the continuing violence that had taken over France.

One of the accounts most read by the British was that of Henry Essex Edgeworth, an English priest who was living in France. Edgeworth was present at the gruesome execution of King Louis XVI, and

The Luddites

The Industrial Revolution resulted in a number of goods made more affordable for the consumer. But those changes did not please everyone, especially the skilled workers—sometimes known as artisans—who had been replaced by machines run by unskilled workers. The most hostile of these artisans (called Luddites) engaged in acts of destruction, smashing mechanized looms and frames in the hope that the new machines would not be replaced and they would get their jobs back.

The Luddite movement received its name from a mythical figure named Ned Ludd. Historians point out that Ludd was supposed to have come from Nottingham, the same part of England that was home to the legendary Robin Hood. According to the legend, Ludd urged skilled artisans to continue causing disruptions until the factories agreed to shut down their steam-powered equipment. However, the violence sometimes turned on the factory owners, one of whom was murdered by the Luddites. That murder infuriated other factory owners, who demanded police action against the Luddites.

By 1814 more than twenty-five Luddites had been apprehended, tried, and hanged for their actions. Not surprisingly, the Luddite movement died out soon afterward—but the term is still used in the twenty-first century to refer to anyone who is opposed to new technology.

his eyewitness description of the event, as well as the crowd's delighted reaction, was especially frightening to the British aristocracy:

> The procession lasted almost two hours; the streets were lined with citizens, all armed, some with pikes and some with guns,

and the carriage was surrounded by a body of troops, formed of the most desperate people of Paris. . . . I feared for a moment that [the King's] courage might fail . . . they dragged him under the axe of the guillotine, which with one stroke severed his head from his body. All this passed in a moment.

The youngest of the guards, who seemed about eighteen, immediately seized the head, and showed it to the people as he walked round the scaffold; he accompanied this monstrous ceremony with the most atrocious and indecent gestures. At first an awful silence prevailed; at length some cries of "Vive la Republique!" [Long live the Republic] were heard. By degrees the voices multiplied and in less than ten minutes this cry, a thousand times repeated, became the universal shout of the multitude, and every hat was in the air.[9]

Nervousness About a British Revolution

Decades after the French Revolution had ended, some in Britain continued to scoff at the ideals that had led to it. In the early nineteenth century the concept of a democracy, in which common people were allowed to own land and vote, was frightening to the British upper classes. English politician Edmund Burke was dismissive of the rights of the masses, insisting that democracy and equal rights were dangerous concepts that went against British values. "The very idea of the fabrication of a new government," Burke writes, "is enough to fill us with disgust and horror."[10]

Some politicians, such as Thomas Macaulay, went even further. Macaulay believed that the idea of even allowing all British citizens the right to vote was too repugnant to consider. He predicted that in a democracy, the first thing people would do "would be to plunder every man in the kingdom who had a good coat on his back and a good roof over his head."[11]

Burke and Macaulay were certainly not alone in their disgust. And many who agreed with them worried that such radical ideas and the violence they had led to in France could spread to England. In his book *The*

Victorian Frame of Mind Walter E. Houghton notes that "for all its solid and imposing strength, Victorian society . . . was shot through, from top to bottom, with the dread of some wild outbreak of the masses that would overthrow the established order and confiscate private property."[12]

For many, France was a lesson in what could happen if the members of the upper class let their guard down, even for a minute. "The lesson," notes Victorian era expert A.N. Wilson, "was simple enough: start to dabble with religious freethinkers, or to question the aristocratic system, and before long you find a guillotine erected; you find kings having their heads chopped off."[13]

A Structured Society

The idea of a British mob rising up against the aristocracy and the monarchy was not entirely far-fetched, for Britain's class system in the years leading up to Victoria's reign was stiflingly rigid. At the top was the royal family, composed of the monarch and his or her family members. Directly under them in the social hierarchy were the upper classes, made up of the wealthy landowners—the aristocracy and the landed gentry. The difference between the two was the source of their holdings: The aristocracy had inherited their land and wealth—and also titles passed down from their fathers. The gentry, on the other hand, had bought their land and acquired wealth through their own efforts.

Next was the middle class, which made up about 15 percent of the population. Middle-class workers ranged from well-to-do bankers to shopkeepers. And finally, at the bottom of the social and economic ladder were the poorest of the English—the working class. They were the laborers, the ones who did the physical work to keep the factories and farms productive. About 70 percent of the people belonged to the working class a decade before Victoria became queen. The poverty most of them endured was severe, and there was little hope for improvement since they had no representation in government.

The only people who had representation in Parliament, Britain's legislative body, were males who owned a considerable amount of land. In addition, the voting districts were skewed in favor of the wealthiest

Privileged spectators attend the coronation of King George IV, a lavish event that cost more than hundreds of average workers could ever hope to earn over their lifetimes. He was an extravagant spender and an unpopular king.

landowners: A man who owned land in several boroughs could vote multiple times. And there were many "rotten boroughs," so called because very few people lived in them. This meant that a single landholder, who might be the only one allowed to vote in that borough, could determine the outcome of an election. Many of the cities that had ballooned in size due to the Industrial Revolution had no representation at all, since they were primarily made up of middle and lower classes.

Although the rigid structure of society was well established, in the early 1830s the working class lashed out at Parliament and King William IV for what they saw as unfair treatment. Their long hours and low wages were unjust, and because they had no representation in

Parliament, there was little hope for change. To emphasize their anger, many workers rioted in the streets in 1831 and again in 1832.

Some lawmakers understood the feelings of frustration. Lord John Russell proposed a bill in Parliament calling for an end to some of the rotten boroughs and allowing more representation of large cities like Birmingham, Leeds, and Manchester. But the bill was voted down twice. However, the third time it was presented one aristocrat reminded King William IV of the dangers of ignoring the working class—evidenced by the revolutions in other countries. "The spirit of the age is triumphing and to resist it is certain destruction,"[14] he told the king.

Thus, the Reform Bill of 1832 was signed. Most of the rotten borough seats were eliminated, and 125 new seats were added in their place. No one can say for certain whether Britain would have suffered its own political revolution had the bill not passed. But historian Simon Jenkins calls the year 1832 "one of the great turning points of England's history."[15]

Victoria's Disappointing Predecessors

Another condition that would have a positive effect on Victoria's reign was the dismal performance of her three predecessors on the throne. As British historian Sir Charles Petrie explains, "If a monarch is to be the effective representative of the nation, he or she must, in a civilized society, be the object of respect."[16] Unfortunately for Britain, however, the three men who ruled Britain before Victoria commanded very little respect.

Her grandfather, George III, was immensely unpopular. During his reign the American colonies fought a successful war against Britain to gain their independence—an event that both disappointed and embarrassed the British people. In the last part of his life George III appeared to be insane, though modern researchers believe he actually suffered from a blood disease called porphyria. He had frequent seizures, hallucinations, and episodes of severe anxiety, which made him unable to function as king. His son George was next in the line of succession and ruled as regent—a substitute for an incapacitated monarch—until his father died, then succeeded him as king.

Queen Victoria and her husband, Prince Albert, appear here with five of their children. Victoria's subjects were pleased to see their young queen marry just a few years after she took the throne.

George IV was even more disappointing than his father. He was an extravagant spender, repeatedly finding ways to get Parliament to loan him money so that he could carry on his lavish lifestyle, which included paying off sizable gambling debts. He was a heavy drinker and was likely addicted to laudanum, a derivative of opium. He was greatly disliked by his subjects, who for the most part lived in dire poverty and resented the small fortune he spent on rebuilding Windsor Castle and redecorating Buckingham Palace. In fact, he planned his own lavish coronation ceremony costing £240,000 (£ is the symbol for British pounds). This was a vast sum for the time period—far more than the combined salaries of hundreds of clerks over their lifetimes. Not surprisingly, he was booed and jeered when he appeared in public, so he tended not to do so very often.

Another of Victoria's uncles, William, succeeded George IV. William was not mad, nor did he spend exorbitant amounts of money on gambling and redecorating. But he did nothing at all to inspire respect for the throne. Although he was married, he fathered ten children with his mistress, a London actress. Like George IV, he was a heavy drinker. He enjoyed the pomp and ceremony of being king but seemed uninterested in affairs of state or the problems plaguing his people.

A Sense of Optimism

Perhaps because of the intense disappointment with the previous monarchs, Victoria's accession to the throne was viewed with great optimism. Though she was young and inexperienced when she became queen, she was also extremely eager to do well.

As English historian Lawrence James explains, Victoria was the first monarch in many years to demonstrate very early in her reign a personal commitment to do well by the people of her empire—which must have pleased many of the people of Britain:

> She is a deeply religious woman, and she sees herself as a Christian ruler over a Christian people, and leading them by moral example. . . . She sees she has a kind of moral duty to look after her people. Almost in the way . . . a benevolent squire might look after his peasants. She has this sort of interest in their daily lives, their everyday lives. And also . . . she shows us throughout her reign [that] she makes no differentiation amongst her subjects. Whether they're English, Scottish, Australian, African or Indian, she sees them as part . . . of [an] extended family of which she is the matriarch.[17]

The British people were relieved, too, when the young queen married her cousin Albert of Saxe-Coburg-Gotha in 1840. The couple had their first child, a daughter, the following year, and in time there would be eight more children. The royal family seemed loving and secure, completely removed from the debauchery and neglect that had characterized the reigns of her predecessors.

However, many insiders in Britain must have wondered whether their fresh-faced new queen's enthusiasm and interest would be enough to keep Britain and its empire safe and prosperous. Eagerly they waited and watched to see what would unfold.

Chapter 2

The Working-Class Life

The Victorian era was a time of enormous contrasts. The Industrial Revolution had resulted in so much progress that it seemed that life would be better for everyone. The new technology did in fact greatly benefit a segment of the population. New methods of farming and manufacturing resulted in a great deal of wealth for the upper and middle classes—people who owned farmland and who built and managed factories.

But however optimistic the lower-class workers were when they moved en masse to the cities to work in factory jobs, their dreams soon evaporated. Most of them learned very quickly that being employed did not necessarily mean that their lives would improve. In fact, for many of them life became much worse.

A Difficult Transition

The workers who moved to large cities like Manchester or London encountered changes that made the transition from farm life very difficult. One was the need to tell time—something most working-class people had never before been required to do. After all, back on the farms, all they needed to know about the passage of time was that when the sun rose, they worked, and when it got dark at night, they slept. Clocks and pocket watches were expensive luxuries that only the upper classes used with regularity. But factories ran on twelve-hour shifts, and employers needed their workers to be on time. As a result, one of the first lessons on the job was learning to read the big clock on the outside of the building.

Another difficult transition for displaced workers was moving from towns or farms to the cramped, crowded slums to which they were relegated. It was quickly apparent that the infrastructures of big cities could not accommodate the rising number of people. The parts of the city where the poorest workers lived were the oldest and most run-down. There was little space for large families, and privacy was non-existent. A family considered itself lucky if it could afford to rent a single shabby room where sometimes six or seven shared a bed—often infested with insects and mice.

Stories abounded of dreadful living conditions. One missionary who visited a poor family in London was appalled at the rooms they and other working-class people were forced to accept, writing that "bugs and fleas and other vermin abound . . . whilst visiting at night I have sometimes seen numbers of bugs coursing over my clothes and hat . . . the stenches have sometimes been so bad that I have been compelled to retreat."[18]

An Unsanitary Life

Even worse than the cramped quarters, however, was the ever present pollution—evident in the clouds of black smoke belching from factories; the soupy, dirty-yellow fog that blanketed industrial cities; and the stink of the water in the nearby rivers. In London, for example, most of the houses had no toilets and no access to reliable sewers. Families kept what were known as "slop jars" in which human waste was collected, and they simply dumped the jars into the river when they were filled. The effect was what historians say was a virtual swamp of filth in the city's water.

The River Thames was a prime example, with 278,000 tons (252,197 metric tons) of untreated sewage daily being dumped into the water—garbage, chemicals and other pollution from factories; the bloated carcasses of dogs, horses, and cattle; and the ever growing amount of human waste. Henry Mayhew, a Victorian sociologist who studied the poorest people in London, reported on the shocking state of the Thames—the source of drinking water for a slum section of South London called Jacob's Island:

An underground train station in London during the Victorian era bustles with activity. The influx of people from the countryside strained the resources of London and other English cities.

In the bright light [the Thames] appeared the colour of strong green tea, and positively looked as solid as black marble . . . indeed, it was more like watery mud than muddy water, and yet we were assured this was the only water which the wretched inhabitants had to drink. As we gazed in horror at it, we saw drains and sewers emptying their filthy contents into it; we saw a whole tier of doorless privies in the open road, open to men and women, built over [the river]; we heard bucket after bucket of filth splash into it.[19]

On one of the rare occasions that Victoria journeyed through the squalor of the working-class neighborhoods around London's factories, she was astonished at how different they were from the rest of the city. She once remarked in her journal how disturbed she was that working-class people had to live in such conditions, noting, "It is another world. In the midst of so much wealth, there seems to be nothing but chimneys, flaring furnaces with wretched cottages around them. Add to this a thick and black atmosphere and you have but a first impression of the life which a third of my subjects are forced to lead."[20]

The Smallest Laborers

Despite the conditions, even a single small room in such dismal neighborhoods was a drain on a working-class income. As a result, most parents found it necessary to put their children to work. In fact, as Victorian scholar David Cody notes, "The displaced working classes, from the seventeenth century on, took it for granted that a family would not be able to support itself if the children were not employed."[21]

Many factory machines did not require strength to run, so employers often preferred to hire women and children to do the work—at a fraction of the small salary they would pay men. Throughout Victorian England, the small stature of a child could be valuable to a company or tradesman. For example, during the Victorian era smaller children were often hired in textile factories to climb behind or underneath heavy machinery, either to clean it or to unravel snarls that slowed production.

In coal mines, children as young as four or five years old could find work as "trappers"; they would occasionally be told to open a trap, a small door to allow fresh air from above ground to circulate in the mine. A trapper's shift might be as long as twelve hours a day, waiting in a narrow, cramped space in the dark until the miners yelled for the child to open the trap. Older children, and sometimes women, were put in harnesses and used as coal hurriers. Their job was to pull heavy tubs of coal through the confusing maze of narrow mine passageways to the surface. Any children who fell asleep at their jobs, as some trappers did when left alone for hours in the dark, were beaten and usually fired.

Crossing Sweepers, Toshers, and Mud Larks

Thousands of enterprising children—and some adults—created their own jobs that sometimes earned them more money than those in mines, mills, or apprenticeships. Some loitered outside offices or pubs

Climbing Boys

One of the most difficult of the children's jobs was that of a "climbing boy," who worked with a chimney sweep to remove the sooty buildup coating the inside of chimneys so that it would not catch fire. Because most chimneys tapered at the top—often a dimension of 9 inches (23 cm) square—the sweeps themselves were too big to reach the narrow upper part of the chimney. For those jobs, they hired climbing boys, as young as four years old.

Simply training to be a climbing boy was staggeringly difficult. Because of the stuffy conditions and tiny spaces in chimneys, the job meant working naked. A Nottingham master chimney sweep named Ruff explains what young boys had to endure as the chimney sweep toughened them up physically in order to perform their backbreaking work:

> No one knows the cruelty which a boy has to undergo in learning. The flesh must be hardened. This is done by rubbing it, chiefly on the elbows and knees, with the strongest brine [salt water] close by a hot fire. You must stand over them with a cane, or coax them with the promise of a halfpenny . . . if they will stand a few more rubs. At first they will come back from their work with their arms and knees streaming with blood, and the knees looking as if the caps had been pulled off; then they must be rubbed with brine again.

Quoted in K.H. Strange, *The Climbing Boys: A Study of Sweeps' Apprentices, 1773–1875*. London: Allison & Busby, 1982, p. 14.

and offered to deliver messages for wealthy businessmen. Also common were the crossing sweepers, who might earn a few pennies a day sweeping a path across an intersection, clearing away as much as possible of the mud and horse manure so well-to-do pedestrians could cross the street without ruining their shoes. In return, the sweepers would hold out a palm, hoping for a halfpenny or two.

At any one time, there were an estimated thousand so-called toshers among the unemployed in London during Victorian times. These were people, usually children, who searched in the sewers for valuables. A group of three or four might go into the sewers together to reduce the chance of getting lost beneath the streets. Not only were the conditions filthy, the job was dangerous. The sewers were rife with big, fierce sewer rats who did not hesitate to bite the intruders. Even so, the job seemed worth the risks, for sometimes valuables were found—coins that had fallen out of a pocket or even jewelry that had slipped through the grates.

Another invented job was that of the mud larks. These were people of all ages, from little children as young as three or four to the elderly, who bravely walked barefoot through the cold, filthy mud in the shallows of the River Thames. Their goal was to find anything of value in the murky bottom—as one historian notes, "the odd lump of coal, a copper nail, a bit of old iron, or a bone."[22] Almost any of those things could be sold to someone—coal to a man whose room was freezing cold, bones to the man who made fertilizer, and a nail to a carpenter. Though the payoff was usually small, there was always the hope that it might be enough to keep hunger at bay for another day.

The Workhouse

Although working families tried hard to survive on their own, many simply could not make enough to feed themselves or afford shelter, especially during the dank winter months. Notes Emory University professor of history Patrick N. Allitt, "Nearly every working family was just a sickness away from absolute poverty."[23] For those people only one option existed: the workhouse. However, the very word struck fear into the hearts of working-class people. In fact, many Victorians stated openly that they would rather die on the streets than be taken to the workhouse. They had good reason to feel this way.

The workhouse came into being in the early seventeenth century, when the political establishment in Britain felt the churches were shouldering the burden of caring for the poor and destitute while not demanding anything in return for their charity. In 1834 Parliament passed legislation that centralized charity for the poor and homeless. These new laws demanded that every local community, known as a parish, within the city of London provide a workhouse to feed and house the poorest of the city's poor—mostly unemployed workers and their families. And to make certain the poor would not flock to the workhouses in order to get free room and board, the facilities would be as wretched as possible. Suggested one organizer, Reverend H.H. Milman, "The workhouses should be a place of hardship, of coarse fare, of degradation and humility; it should be administered with strictness—with severity; it should be as repulsive as is consistent with humanity."[24]

Fear and Hopelessness

As a result, those who entered the workhouse were treated much like prison inmates. Their clothes and possessions were confiscated, and they were given a standard-issue uniform. Most of the men had their hair shaved to prevent lice. It must have startled the first entrants to the workhouses when they realized that families would not be permitted to live together. Half of the workhouse consisted of dormitories designated for "male paupers" and the other for "female paupers." Children often stayed with the same-sex parent, though the workhouse supervisors had the authority to loan out—and sometimes even sell—a child as an apprentice. Some families were never reunited; husbands never saw their wives again, and boys never saw their sisters or mothers again.

People who witnessed friends or neighbors being taken to the workhouse never forgot the experience. One man told workhouse researcher Jennifer Worth how, when he was doing labor outside a workhouse as a young boy, he saw an old man come up with his wife: "He had a little handkerchief tied round the little things what they had got left, the old girl on his arm was crying her bloody eyes out. She was hanging back as they got up to the big doors [of the workhouse], but the matron got hold of her and took her away, and the master took the poor bloke the other way. That's the last they saw of each other."[25]

Workhouse inmates were expected to work, though the labor was mindless and often purposeless. Some men ground large rocks into smaller bits of gravel, while others picked apart thick rope called oakum into smaller strands, which were then used for caulking ships. Even after the navy stopped using the oakum strands, the workhouse supervisors continued to have inmates do this repetitive, mind-numbing task so they had something to occupy their time. As British historian Sally Mitchell explains, "This labor did not train people for employment: it was simply deterrent, designed to make people think twice about claiming relief."[26]

The dismal conditions and the breakup of families were heartbreaking. However, the alternative was worse—for parents to watch their children go hungry day after day. It is perhaps, then, not so surprising that the workhouses were busy and frequently had to turn people away.

Grisly rumors were repeated about the fate of people sent to workhouses. One workhouse inspector wrote in 1839, "A short time back it was circulated in this county that the children in the workhouses were killed to make pies with, while the old when dead were employed to manure the guardians' fields, in order to save the expense of coffins."[27] While there was no way to substantiate such rumors, the mere fact that they were believable at the time says a great deal about the grim life people led in the workhouses.

Crime in the City

With so much poverty in the cities, it is not surprising that crime was a significant problem during Victorian times. Only about five thousand criminal offenses were reported annually in the early 1800s, but the number had skyrocketed to about twenty thousand by the 1840s. Shoplifting and burglary were common; assaults and murder less so.

More than any other category, juvenile crime saw the most dramatic

A young mother helps her son try on a jacket at a secondhand clothes market. Lack of work forced many newcomers to English cities into poverty. The more fortunate among them could afford used clothing; the rest wore what they had even when those clothes turned to little more than rags.

increase during Victorian times. It was rampant among the poorest of the working class. The contact between seasoned criminals and children, sometimes as young as four or five, often occurred in what were known as "flash-houses"—pubs that were gathering places for a host of criminals. The older criminals frequently recruited boys and girls to whom they would teach the finer points of picking pockets, housebreaking, and other types of theft at which children might be more agile than adults.

In 1839 W.A. Miles of London's Prison Discipline Society wrote that he was particularly troubled by the very young criminal population in London: "[They are] devoted to crime, trained to it from infancy, adhering to it from Education and Circumstances, whose connections prevent the possibility of reformation, and whom no Punishment can deter; . . . [they are] different from the rest of Society, not only in thoughts, habits and manners, but even in appearance, possessing, moreover, a language all their own."[28]

Too Many Convicts

The burgeoning number of youthful offenders was straining the already crowded jails to the breaking point. In fact, British officials had been sending many convicted criminals to their colonies around the world since the seventeenth century, simply because they lacked jail space. Until 1783 when the American colonies were successful in their revolution, Britain had transported many of its convicted felons there. In 1788 Britain began sending them on ships to Australia, where it had established a large penal colony. Over the next eighty years more than 165,000 convicts were sentenced to Australia, chained below the deck for the entire six-month voyage. The lack of fresh air and the abundance of disease in the cramped quarters below deck resulted in up to one-third of the convicts dying en route.

Sometimes no seaworthy ships were ready to take the prisoners to Australia. In these instances, convicts were housed on floating prisons, known as hulks, to wait until such ships became available. Convicts of all ages were imprisoned on hulks. This meant that in addition to living in cramped and filthy conditions, the youngest and smallest inmates— some as young as ten or eleven—were often bullied and victimized by older ones.

The victims tried mightily to get taken off a hulk—even injuring themselves on purpose to be transferred to a hospital. One man worked as a medic at a hospital that accepted patients from a hulk called the *Euryalus*. He explains to what lengths the boys would go to escape the ship:

I have known the Boys take an old Copper Button and apply it hot to the Skin, then apply Soap and Rum to a Sore occasioned by a hot Button, and wrap it up for Two or Three Days and then show that wound to the Doctor, and then come to the Hospital in a State piteous to behold. . . . I have several Cases in which they have broken the Arms to get into the Hospital; they held the Arms upon a [hard surface] and let the edge of the table drop upon them to break [the arm] in two.[29]

Scandal in the Workhouse

Historians say it is difficult to exaggerate the cruelty of Victorian-era workhouses. But most people had no idea how bad conditions were until a scandal in the Andover workhouse in Hampshire was brought to light in 1845. Journalists revealed that inmates at Andover were starving because the manager of the workhouse was appropriating food supplies for his own use.

One of the jobs workhouse inmates did was grind bones from slaughterhouses into fragments to make fertilizer. However, there were reports that some of the inmates at Andover were so hungry that they were fighting over some of the cattle, horse, dog, and other animal bones. One official of the district was told by some of the paupers from the workhouse that the rotten meat from those bones was an acquired taste, but men would fight over the bones.

Recalls the official, "They said that when one found . . . a fresh bone, one that appeared a little moist, that they were almost ready to fight over it, and that the man who was fortunate enough to get it was obliged to hide it that he might eat it when he was alone."

Quoted in Norman Longmate, *The Workhouse*. New York: St. Martin's, 1974.

Increasing Calls for Reforms

From the swelling crime rate and the lack of well-paying jobs to the general squalor of their communities, the problems of the large working class were an ever present reminder that Britain had enormous domestic problems. And because the working class had no representation in Parliament, it seemed unlikely that these problems would be solved anytime soon.

Although the middle class had received more government representation with the passage the Reform Act of 1832, the working class had not. Poverty, disease, and crime remained rife in their neighborhoods. And while Parliament had passed legislation in 1833 limiting the hours children could work in factories and mines, it had done nothing for the deplorable working conditions of their parents.

In 1838, one year after Victoria ascended the throne, a working-class protest group known as the Chartists presented a list of demands to Parliament, including the right for all adults to vote and a system in which members of Parliament (MPs) received pay, so that even poor people could afford to run for office. Though the British government symbolically passed laws agreeing to the demands, in reality they merely ignored them, and nothing changed. A decade later the Chartist movement had fizzled out due to a lack of leadership within its ranks.

Changes at Last

By the late 1840s, however, things had begun to change. Although Parliament was still dominated by the upper class, some members had become more open to the idea of reforms. The issue of education was one of the first to be addressed. For many years schools had been the domain of the wealthy. The children of the working class had almost no access to schools because even the youngest children were needed to work. But throughout the nineteenth century, employers experienced a need for more skilled workers who could at least read and do arithmetic. Responding to that need, Parliament passed education bills in 1870 and 1880 that required all children to attend school at least until age eleven.

During this time two pieces of legislation were most heartening to the workers. The first was a reform bill passed in 1867 that allowed more than 1.5 million men to vote—many of them in the urban working class. The second was the Trade Union Act of 1871. It allowed workers to unionize so that they could appoint leaders, organize, and negotiate with employers to gain better working conditions, higher salaries, and other concessions.

By the end of the nineteenth century, not only were most working-class men able to vote, but a few of their peers were sitting in Parliament. As Victorian scholar Richard D. Altick notes, these new members of Parliament "were curiosities, but no longer absolute rarities. The old order had changed indeed, yielding place to new."[30]

Chapter 3

Science and Technology in the Victorian Era

The Industrial Revolution had spawned a great many new inventions that had an enormous effect on people's lives. Besides delighting many of the first passengers, the introduction of railways throughout Britain connected the towns and cities of the island in a way that they had never been linked before. In fact, for many years, people simply did not even consider traveling within Britain because it was incredibly difficult and time-consuming. Roads were in poor condition, and there were few bridges over the island's many rivers and streams.

Charles Petrie quotes a 1752 article in England's *The Gentleman's Magazine* in which the writer explains, "A rich citizen of London has perhaps some very valuable relations or friends in the West [of England]; he thinks no more of visiting them than of traveling the deserts of Nubia [an area near the Nile River in Africa], which might as well be on the moon."[31]

A Whole New Life

But within a decade of the passenger train's debut, there were more than five thousand miles of track connecting English cities and towns. For the first time in the nation's history it was possible to board a train, go to a town or city to visit a relative or to shop, and return home the same day—something unimaginable just decades before. Prince

Albert was amazed at how much faster the trip was from London to the port of Bristol, on England's west coast. The 120-mile trip (193 km) that used to take him fifteen hours by stagecoach took only three hours on the train.

One railroad passenger who traveled to Birmingham from London in 1838 was even more amazed at how pleasurable traveling by train could be. He enthusiastically predicted that the new mode of transportation would do much for the people of Britain: "This morning I set out per railroad. . . . Of six whom the coach contained, I knew three. We talked [about] Magnetism and I read [chapter] III of Nicholas Nickleby [a novel by Charles Dickens], very amusing and in one part powerfully written. I think railroads will go far towards making us a more social people. There is more chance of meeting gentlefolks than in the old [stagecoach] system."[32]

Fresh Food and National Sports

Railroads also added to people's quality of life. There were no refrigerators or freezers to keep food fresh, so those in the city had always eaten foods that were preserved, dried, or pickled instead of fresh fruits and vegetables. But railways were a cheap, fast way for farmers to get their produce to markets in cities and towns. As a result, city dwellers suddenly had access to a vast range of healthy food they had rarely been able to buy before.

Interestingly, railroads can also be credited with the explosive growth of Britain's sports leagues. For many years teams had competed in popular games such as football (known as soccer in the United States), rugby, and cricket. But because travel was difficult and time-consuming, teams were almost always limited to competing with teams from the same area, often according to their own local rules. As a result, there were no standardized regulations for games.

But with the coming of the railroads, a team could travel to compete against teams from anywhere in Britain, and their fans could travel to watch. Tournaments could be scheduled and leagues set up and regulated, so teams hundreds of miles apart could compete for national championships. In 1888 Britain's first professional sports organization, the Football Association, was formed—something that would never have been thought possible just decades before.

The Steamship

The Victorian era also saw the first steam engines used to power large seagoing ships. Up until this time, ships were powered by wind—a definite drawback for a nation like Britain, with so many colonies around the world making up its sizable empire. Sailing ships depended entirely on currents and the direction of the wind, and as a result, it was impossible to estimate accurately how long a voyage might last. In the days of sailing ships, the trip from England to Canada or America would take at least three months. To go from England to one of its most valuable colonies, India, would take six months or more.

However, the age of steam eventually resulted in a new type of travel—the steamship. The first steam engines were used on small boats to run wooden paddle wheels. But an English inventor and engineer named Isambard Kingdom Brunel was the first to design an iron ship—bigger than any existing ship in the world—that could run entirely on steam. In fact, the SS *Great Britain*, as he named it, was double the size of any previous ship.

Critics mocked Brunel's ideas, for it was widely believed in those days that a heavy iron steamship of that size would require so much coal for its engines that there would be no space for cargo. However, Brunel was sure of himself because he had a good understanding of both mathematics and buoyancy. To his critics he presented a complex mathematical equation that demonstrated that the bigger the ship, the more room there would be for passengers or cargo.

The *Great Britain* moved in a straight line, as Brunel intended, without the crew worrying about variances in wind or current. As a result, the steamship shaved about ten weeks from the length of a sailing ship's time to reach North America. Because voyages by steamship were so much faster than sailing voyages, it became easier for Britain to maintain a tighter control over its empire.

Science and the Public's Health

In addition to technological advances, there were significant scientific breakthroughs during the Victorian era. Several of these were beneficial to the public's health, including advances made in dealing with dangerous diseases—including the most feared disease in the nineteenth century: cholera.

Nearly one hundred thousand people died of cholera during Victoria's reign. Within a day of exhibiting the first symptoms, a victim would be dead, and sometimes within only a few hours. Though cholera struck infants and the elderly most frequently, anyone could catch it, and it spread quickly. It was, according to historian Roy Porter, a horrible way to die, for a victim grew dizzy and nauseated, and suffered horrible diarrhea and extreme muscle cramps: "[There was] an insatiable desire for water, followed by a 'sinking stage' during which the pulse dropped and lethargy set in. Dehydrated and near death, the patient displayed the classic cholera physiognomy: puckered blue lips in a cadaverous face. There was no agreement about its cause; many treatments were tried; nothing worked."[33]

At the time there was no real understanding of the presence of germs that could be responsible for causing disease. Instead, many believed that cholera, like other diseases, was caused by "miasma," or bad air. The theory was that particularly foul odors, such as those emanating from garbage, stagnant water, or human or animal waste, contained particles that when inhaled would cause diseases.

According to Victorian public health advocate Edwin Chadwick, the poor were far more likely to have—and spread—cholera because their sense of smell had somehow diminished, and they did not close their windows, so the miasma quickly infected them. As he explains: "The sense of smell . . . which generally give certain warning of the presence of . . . gases noxious to the health, appears often to be obliterated in the labourer by his employment . . . there is scarcely any stench which is not endured to avoid slight cold . . . these adverse circumstances tend to produce an adult population short-lived, improvident, reckless, and intemperate."[34]

Urban Centers of Victorian England, 1861

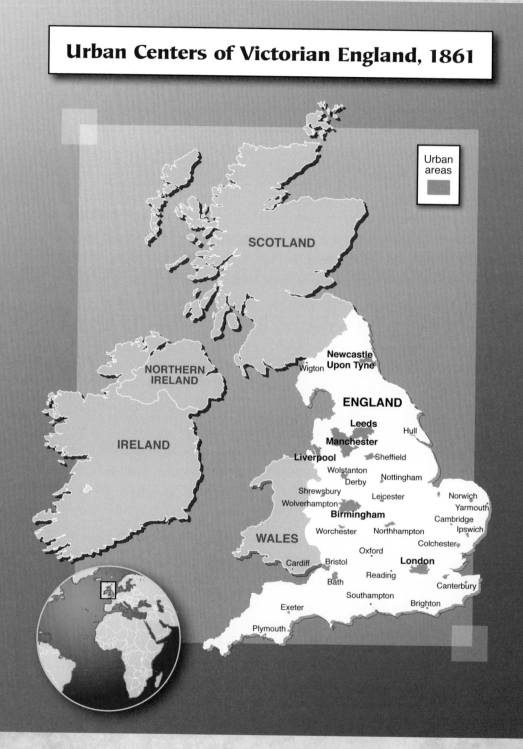

Urban areas

SCOTLAND

NORTHERN IRELAND

IRELAND

Newcastle Upon Tyne

Wigton

ENGLAND

Leeds

Hull

Manchester

Liverpool

Sheffield

Wolstanton

Derby

Nottingham

Shrewsbury

Leicester

Norwich

Yarmouth

Wolverhampton

Birmingham

Cambridge

Ipswich

WALES

Worcester

Northhampton

Colchester

Oxford

Cardiff

Bristol

London

Bath

Reading

Canterbury

Southampton

Brighton

Exeter

Plymouth

Finding the Source of a Cholera Outbreak

The fear of cholera diminished greatly because of the work of physician John Snow. He did not believe that whatever caused cholera was inhaled but suggested that the disease perhaps was spread when a healthy person unknowingly ingested the excretions [waste products] of someone infected with the disease.

In 1854, after a cholera outbreak on Broad Street in a part of London called Soho, Snow suggested that the water pump in the area around the first victims' homes be inspected, as well as the drain and the well below it to see whether neighborhood sewage somehow was leaking into the well. After a thorough inspection, workers found that the cesspool under the house of the first victim, a baby, was indeed in bad repair. It was crumbling, and when the baby's mother had washed out a dirty diaper, the baby's waste had subsequently leaked into the well that supplied the neighborhood with water.

Snow ordered the pump handle on Broad Street removed so others would not be able to get water from that location and put themselves at risk of getting the disease. Though many of Snow's fellow physicians were skeptical of his theory, the results showed he was right. Once people began using other pumps in the city, there were no new cases in the Broad Street area.

Reducing Infection

Another breakthrough in medicine occurred during the late nineteenth century, when Joseph Lister proved that many dangerous infections after surgery could be prevented. Until then, doctors believed that infections were simply part of the normal healing process. Doctors rarely washed their hands between seeing patients, nor did it even cross their minds to clean instruments or the white coats they wore, for they did not believe there was any reason to. The "good old surgical stink," as doctors referred to the smell at the site of a patient's surgery—and on their own coats— was not considered problematic. As medical journalist Victor Robinson writes, the amount of bodily fluids on a doctor's coat was a point of pride:

Coffins for the Undead

The Victorians had two fears involving death. The first was having the corpse stolen by grave robbers and sold to a teaching hospital to be dissected by medical students. This fear was well founded and resulted in families standing vigil over a loved one's grave for several days—after that, it was reasoned, the body would be so decayed that it would be unusable.

The second fear was that of being mistakenly pronounced dead while merely in a coma, and then buried alive. To address this fear, in 1852 an English inventor named George Bateson created what became known as the "Bateson's Belfry," a coffin that could prevent such a catastrophe. It was made with a miniature bell tower on the lid, complete with an iron bell. A thin rope on the bell was attached to the finger of the deceased through a small hole in the coffin lid. If the person revived while in the coffin, the person need only pull on the string and the sound of the bell would alert someone above ground. Queen Victoria bestowed a medal on Bateson for service to the dead.

"Every surgeon was proud of his old operating coat which he neither washed nor changed, for the accumulating incrustations of dried blood and pus attested to his experience. Operators and their assistants . . . came from autopsies or the dissecting-room, and without cleaning their hands, examined patients and parturient [birthing] women."[35]

It is easy to understand, then, why so many patients died after surgery. In fact, between 1864 and 1866 the fatality rate for patients who had amputations was an astonishing 46 percent. It was during this time that Joseph Lister began experimenting with carbolic acid, a substance known to remove odors, as a means of preventing infections in the operating room. At the time, Lister was working at a large hospital in

Glasgow, Scotland. Lister was aware of French researcher Louis Pasteur's new findings concerning germs as a cause of disease and believed carbolic acid could help keep the germs from infecting wounds.

Lister began spraying surgical instruments with a mixture of carbolic acid and water. He also used the same mixture to wash his hands before operating on or examining a patient. He also began using carbolic acid on the dressings and even on the surgical incisions themselves. His idea was a good one, and the rate of infected amputations in Victorian hospitals plummeted as other doctors began following his example.

Dulling Pain

The Victorian era also ushered in the use of safer anesthetics during surgery. Many people in the nineteenth century were terrified to have surgery because of the severe pain involved. Notes historian Liza Picard, "A surgeon's success rate . . . had largely depended on his dexterity in completing an operation so fast that the patient hardly had time to feel the pain, until post operative-pain hit him later."[36] In the early part of the Victorian era, doctors were limited to using either opium or alcohol as anesthesia—both of which could be very risky for the patient.

In the 1840s physician James Simpson of Edinburgh, Scotland, had been experimenting with a chemical called chloroform that seemed to be a promising alternative. Unlike alcohol, it was not flammable, nor did it seem to have adverse effects in patients if used in moderation. A patient would remain conscious but feel no pain after inhaling just a few drops on a handkerchief. According to one often told story, Simpson and several of his medical students were at his home discussing chloroform as they waited for dinner to be served. One of the students accidently upset the bottle of chloroform, and when Simpson's wife came into the room to announce that dinner was ready, she found everyone on the floor, sound asleep from the chemical.

Victoria herself was one of the earliest to take advantage of chloroform. Historians say the queen had a very low pain threshold and as a result suffered intensely giving birth to her first seven children. On April 7, 1853, she went into labor with her eighth child, Leopold. Her physician was John Snow—the same man who, months later, would discover the source of the cholera epidemic. He administered chloroform during the birth—which the queen found amazingly pleasant. Later she remarked that "the effect was soothing, quieting, and delightful beyond measure."[37]

Previously, women had been uncomfortable with the idea of being given the new anesthetic, but after the queen's experience, many women of the aristocracy followed Victoria's lead. Soon, the use of chloroform became common during a range of medical procedures. However, many religious leaders condemned the use of the anesthetic in labor. They insisted that the Bible was very clear that women were intended to suffer pain during childbirth, quoting a verse in which God tells Eve that "in sorrow thou shalt bring forth children."[38]

Charles Darwin's Theory

Not every scientific discovery of the Victorian era had immediate practical uses. In fact, one of the most groundbreaking scientific accomplishments was a book written in 1858 by naturalist Charles Darwin titled *On the Origin of Species by Means of Natural Selection*. Darwin had been fascinated by the work of geologist Charles Lyell, who had found fossils of dinosaurs that were believed to be millions or even billions of years old. This idea collided head-on with the Christian wisdom of the time—a literal view of the Bible that said God created the world in six days, just about six thousand years ago.

When Darwin participated in a five-year expedition that explored the coasts of South America and the Galapagos Islands, he found evidence suggesting that earth was, in fact, far older than Christians believed. Darwin also found evidence to reinforce his idea of evolution: Plants and animals, including humans, of the time were not the same as they had been thousands or even millions of years ago. They had changed over the eons in ways that had allowed them to better adapt to their environments.

Darwin's idea of evolution was roundly debated by the scientific community as well as by church officials. Some were excited about the ideas contained in the book, while others condemned it outright. Though he was confident in his findings, Darwin also believed that the

The Speed of the Railway

In her book *Victorian London: The Tale of a City, 1840–1870*, Liza Picard discusses the effects of the higher rate of speed experienced by the railroad's customers in the early Victorian era. It was, she explains, a velocity none had ever imagined.

The speed of a railway train was terrifying. When Queen Victoria was whisked from Slough (the nearest station to Windsor Castle, then) to London in 1842, the train averaged 44 m.p.h. over the 17-mile journey, and she asked Albert to tell the railway company that she had not enjoyed it, please go more slowly in future. Yet the engines displayed at the Great Exhibition by the North Western Railway . . . had "taken trains at speeds . . . from 60 to 70 miles an hour," [according to Dionysius Lardner, a quoted source].

Could the human body survive the pressure of such velocity? It had never before been subjected to such a strain; until the railway age, the fastest anyone had traveled was on a galloping horse, and the speed of a stagecoach was reckoned to be as fast as anyone would want to go. *Bradshaw's Railway Timetables*, which had been available since 1839, reckoned on an average speed of express trains of 36–48 m.p.h. Before the advent of the railway, peaceful country towns had set their clocks by whatever time-keeping system they chose. Because of Bradshaw, for the first time ever, Englishmen all over the country could synchronise their watches.

Liza Picard, *Victorian London: The Tale of a City, 1840–1870*. New York: St. Martin's, 2005, p. 34.

The Crystal Palace, immense in size and ornate in its décor, housed an international exhibition in London in 1851. Prince Albert saw the exhibition as an opportunity for countries around the world to display their scientific and technological accomplishments.

concept of evolution and a belief in God were compatible. He writes: "There is grandeur in this view of life, with its several powers having been originally breathed into a few forms or into one; and that, whilst this planet had gone cycling on according to the fixed law of gravity, from so simple a beginning endless forms most beautiful and most wonderful have been, and are being evolved."[39]

But many disagreed and were furious that Darwin's science undermined what they believed were truths contained in the Old Testament.

How, they wondered, could the notion that man was descended from apes not be contradictory to the Bible that claimed God gave man dominion over all the animals? The debate has raged into the twenty-first century between those who believe Darwin's theories of evolution and those who object to the teaching of evolution as a science.

The Great Exhibition

During the Victorian era there was great pride and optimism among the British for the progress being made in technology, science, and manufacturing. In this spirit, Albert suggested that Britain hold a large trade fair, or exhibition, to showcase those accomplishments. But unlike similar exhibitions that had been held in other European countries, such as Germany and France, this would be an international gathering that would allow nations around the world to demonstrate their progress and accomplishments, too. The outcome, the prince hoped, would further international relations and understanding.

To house the event, the official name of which would be "The Great Exhibition of the Works of Industry of All Nations," a beautiful building was erected in Hyde Park, London. Known as the Crystal Palace, the structure was immense—1,851 feet (564 m) long and tall enough to cover several full-grown elm trees already growing in the park. It was made of almost three hundred thousand panes of glass connected by iron rods. The Crystal Palace itself was hailed as an immense accomplishment. Even years later, one British aristocrat remembered how overcome he was when he saw it for the first time: "[It] was so graceful, so delicate, so airy that its translucent beauty remains graven on my memory, as something that must defy all rivalry. When I first saw it glittering in the morning sun, I felt as if Aladdin and the genie that was the slave of the lamp must have been at work on it. No mere human hands could have worked such a miracle."[40]

The Best of the Best

But it was the exhibits within the Crystal Palace that excited the more than 6 million visitors. During the exhibition's 141-day run, visitors browsed among almost a hundred thousand exhibits that demonstrated the newest and most exciting inventions and accomplishments from throughout the world.

They viewed a chunk of gold ore from the recent California gold rush, furs from Canada, and Mathew Brady's groundbreaking work in photography. They saw the largest diamond in the world—the 186-carat Koh-i-Noor from India—as well as several new models of Samuel Colt's revolvers, a sportsman's pocketknife with eighty different blades, and the newly invented gas cooking stove. People also looked with interest at the first yellow pencil, large slabs of Swiss chocolate, and an odd-looking machine that could actually make more than two dozen envelopes in a minute.

One of the most popular exhibits was the telegraph that had been set up inside the Crystal Palace, and visitors stared openmouthed as messages were sent to Edinburgh, and an answer was sent back right away. There were also some less serious exhibits, such as an umbrella that could be used as a defensive weapon and, as Patrick N. Allitt notes, such oddities as "a stuffed frog for holding umbrellas, [and] an alarm clock that actually threw the occupant out of bed when the appropriate moment had come."[41]

The Great Exhibition was an enormous financial success, clearing a profit of £200,000, equivalent to £12,000,000 pounds ($18,480,000) today. But even more exciting to Victoria was the public's glowing praise of Albert. She visited the Crystal Palace more than forty times and insisted each time she was more proud than the last. "I wish you could have witnessed the 1st May 1851 [opening of the Great Exhibition]," she wrote to her Uncle Leopold, the king of Belgium, "the greatest day in our history, the most beautiful and imposing and touching spectacle ever seen, and the triumph of my beloved Albert."[42]

After the Great Exhibition, there was no doubt that the people of Britain had a great deal to be proud of. But as promising as Britain's economic outlook seemed, as it was at the forefront of science and technology, the view of Britain's foreign affairs did not inspire the same sort of pride and optimism.

Chapter 4

Empire Building and Maintenance

When Victoria became queen in 1837, Britain was proud of its vast empire. Since the fifteenth and sixteenth centuries, Britain had been adding colonies throughout the world, including Canada in North America, as well as Ireland, Australia, New Zealand, Bermuda, Sierra Leone, Singapore, and the Cape of Good Hope in South Africa.

Some of Britain's colonies had been acquired by military force, while others were claimed for the British crown by explorers in these territories when they found no official central government in place. Finally, there were a few territories that had actually been settled by private trading companies—most notably India, without a doubt one of Britain's most valuable possessions. At the time Victoria ascended the throne, India was officially under the control of the East India Company, a private English corporation that had been created in 1600 to pursue trade with the East Indies.

By the nineteenth century, Britain was considered a global superpower. It had a navy second to none and was also the world's undisputed industrial leader. However, Victorian Britain was less interested in becoming embroiled in new wars to gain territory than in expanding its economic empire—seeking to establish territories that could supply raw materials for British manufacturers and to find new markets for its goods. Its mighty navy could keep routes open for British trading vessels as well as the ships of Britain's trading partners. However, early in Victoria's reign some of Britain's most difficult challenges were dealing with crises in established parts of its empire.

A Crisis in Ireland

One of its possessions experiencing great problems during the mid-1850s was Ireland, Britain's oldest colony. The English had ruled Ireland since the 1100s, and over the centuries they had made Protestantism Ireland's official religion—though most of the Irish were Catholics. Those Catholics who refused to convert were punished by having their land seized and turned over to English landlords. A typical English landlord usually preferred to remain in England and hire a foreman to manage the laborers who did the physically difficult farmwork.

The system worked well for the wealthy landowner, but resulted in difficult lives for his laborers. In addition to working the farms for the absentee English landlords, many laborers rented small strips of land on which they grew their own food. Most lived in squalid mud huts and often kept a few animals inside with them—a couple of chickens or perhaps a piglet. The latter was sometimes jokingly referred to as "the gentleman who paid the rent" because when the pig was grown, it would be sold for much-needed rent money.

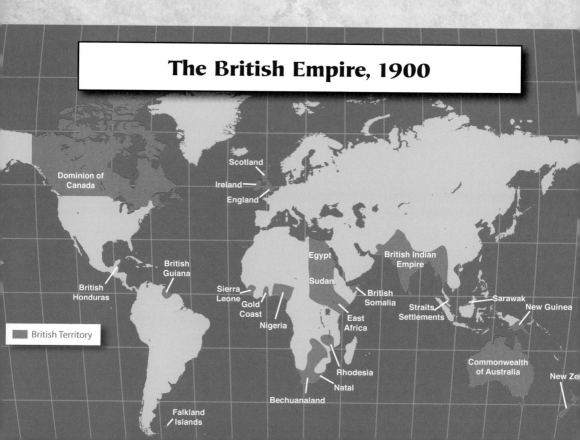

The British Empire, 1900

Dominion of Canada

Scotland

Ireland

England

British Guiana

British Honduras

Egypt

Sudan

British Indian Empire

Sierra Leone

Gold Coast

Nigeria

British Somalia

East Africa

Straits Settlements

Sarawak

New Guinea

Commonwealth of Australia

New Ze

Rhodesia

Natal

Bechuanaland

Falkland Islands

British Territory

Potatoes were the staple food of the laborers—in fact, many of them ate nothing else throughout their entire lives. Potatoes were an easy crop to grow in Ireland, where the weather was rainy and never too hot. The plants were hardy and needed little care, which was convenient, since the laborers were required to spend most of their time tending the landowners' crops. A rented acre-sized plot (0.4 ha) was enough to grow 6 tons (5.4 metric tons) of potatoes each year, which would feed a family of six.

But in 1845 the potato crop failed, blighted by a fungus that turned the potato harvest gummy, black, foul smelling, and completely inedible. In his book *The Graves Are Walking*, John Kelly describes the horror the workers felt when they began harvesting and realized their potato crop had fallen victim to the blight. "In Cork, men wept openly as half-ruined potatoes were lifted from the ground. In Limerick, shovels dropped and laborers soaked through to the skin with rain filed out of the fields like mourners."[43]

The fungus returned with a vengeance the following year and again in 1848. In a culture with a wide variety of foods to eat, a disease attacking one crop might not have been an insurmountable problem. But in Ireland, among the poorest people it was a disaster. Measured by the number of deaths that resulted from it, historians say that the Irish Potato Famine was the worst human disaster of the nineteenth century. Of its population of 8.2 million, Ireland lost an estimated 1.5 million to starvation and disease.

A Starving Land

The eyewitness accounts of the misery were heart wrenching because people were willing to eat virtually anything to keep themselves alive. Many ate grass and seaweed. After a cattle show in Dublin, one witness saw a peasant sneak into the pens to retrieve half-eaten pieces of turnips that cows had been munching on. Another wrote about seeing a man spitting out a gooseberry seed, which was quickly retrieved by a starving woman who gave it to her young child. William Forster, a Quaker, visited County Mayo during the height of the famine and was horrified by the physical change that starvation caused in the youngest victims:

The Terrible Hunger

In his book *Famine Echoes*, Cathal Poirteir includes the memories of the descendants of survivors of the Irish Potato Famine. The following is that of John Doyle, a laborer from County Wicklow, Ireland, who recalls the lengths to which people would go to find anything edible so that they might survive another day.

> The people ate crabapples and holly-berries and the leaves of the crabtree. They climbed trees for nuts in Rednagh [an area of County Wicklow] . . . a favourite was the oak nut [acorn]. Many were so weak they fell out of the trees and were killed. They fought and killed each other over the blackberries before they were ripe. . . . Trees were climbed at night in search of crows and woodquest's [woodpigeon] eggs and they would eat every bird of all descriptions that they could catch.

> A landlord who was afraid that all the birds of the county would be exterminated paid a bounty of [two pennies] for every live bird that was brought to him and he kept them and fed them until after the famine.

> The people around Aughrim had snares for killing mice. They skinned and ate them but never gutted them. One man saw a rat and a weasel fighting and tried to kill both of them but the weasel bit him and he was so weak that the poison from the bite killed him.

Quoted in Cathal Poirteir, *Famine Echoes*. Dublin, IR: Gill and Macmillan, 1995, pp. 59–60.

"We entered a cabin. Stretched in one dark corner, scarcely visible from the smoke and rags that covered them, were three children huddled together, lying there because they were too weak to rise, pale and ghastly;

their little limbs, on removing a portion of the filthy covering, perfectly emaciated, eyes sunk, voice gone, and evidently in the last stage of actual starvation."[44]

As the farmworkers became weak with hunger, they were unable to do their work or pay their rent, and many were evicted from their homes on orders from the English landowners. Between 1846 and 1854 more than half a million workers and their families found themselves homeless. Many of these, already weak from hunger, were easy targets of dysentery, cholera, and other diseases. With little hope of surviving in Ireland, millions left for Canada or America on what came to be known as "coffin ships" because of the numbers who died during the month-long voyage.

Reactions in Britain

The reaction in Britain was inadequate at best. Many wealthy and middle-class people in Britain believed that the Irish were inherently lazy and far less civilized than the English—and therefore probably deserved what was happening to them. In one editorial the London *Times* insisted that the famine might actually be a good thing, for it could teach the Irish to change their diet, and in the process they would become harder workers: "For our parts, we regard the potato blight as a blessing. When the [Irish] once cease to be potato eaters, they must become carnivorous. With the taste of meats will grow the appetite for them; with the appetite, the readiness to earn them. With this will come steadiness, regularity, and perseverance."[45]

Not everyone in England was unsympathetic. Victoria herself sent a large personal donation to an organization working to help the Irish. Robert Peel, the prime minister, wanted to import shipments of American grain that could be distributed to the victims. To do that, it would be necessary to repeal the Corn Laws, which protected the economic interests of British farmers by requiring high taxes to be paid on any grain imported from outside Britain.

Repealing the laws, however, would mean a loss of income for the British landowners, many of whom were members of Parliament. Not surprisingly, they voted to keep the Corn Laws in place.

Eventually the laws were repealed, but it was too late for tens of thousands of Irish families.

Troubles Simmering in India

India was another trouble spot during Victoria's reign. In 1600 British traders had visited India, hoping to find a source of spices and other goods. Spices had great value; aside from enhancing the flavor of food, spices were used in embalming the dead, preserving food, and making perfumes. A trader who could deliver spices in bulk to England would become wealthy in a very short time.

Not only did the people of India have a multitude of exotic spices, but they also had silks and other fabrics to trade. More and more British traders began to do business there, opening trading posts in places such as Burma and the Punjab on the Indian subcontinent. The traders formed a corporation called the East India Company, which by the time of Victoria's reign was essentially ruling large parts of India with the force of its private military—consisting of both British and Indian soldiers—known as the British Indian Army.

When Victoria came to the throne, a group of only thirty thousand British people was presiding over a population of more than 200 million in India. Understandably, there was dissension among many of the Indian people. They were resentful of the British, who seemed to belittle Indian customs and religious rites—apparently with the blessing of the British government.

For example, William Wilberforce, a member of Parliament, strongly encouraged English missionaries to target the people of India because he considered the natives' Hindu religious customs backward. "Our religion is sublime, pure, and beneficial, while theirs is mean, licentious and cruel . . . the most enormous and tormenting superstition that ever harassed and degraded any portion of mankind."[46]

Queen Victoria was not as outwardly critical of the Hindu religion as Wilberforce was. She did, however, express the attitude shared by many Britons when she proclaimed that England's duty was "to protect the poor natives and advance civilization."[47]

The Indian Mutiny

The breaking point with the Indian soldiers in the British Indian Army, known as sepoys, occurred shortly after they were provided with new rifles. The weapons in those days required the shooter to bite open a paper cartridge full of gunpowder and pour the powder into the rifle's muzzle. To keep the cartridge waterproof, the manufacturers coated the paper with grease.

But in 1857, when a rumor began to circulate among the sepoys that these particular cartridges were coated with hog and beef lard, tensions arose. The sepoys' ranks contained both Hindus and Muslims. Hindus considered the cow sacred and thus were not permitted to touch beef fat; Muslims were forbidden to touch pork. The rumors about the cartridges turned out to be correct, and on May 18, 1857, during training exercises, eighty-five of the sepoys refused to fire their rifles. For disobeying an order, British officers promptly put them in leg irons and sentenced them to ten years in jail.

That night, a group of sepoys stormed the jail, released the prisoners, killed the English soldiers, and set fire to the building. They then marched to Delhi and killed hundreds of people, mostly British soldiers and traders as well as their wives and children. "We are in sad anxiety about India, which engrosses all our attention," Victoria writes in a letter to her uncle Leopold. She tells him she is especially bothered by the civilian deaths, writing, "The horrors committed on the poor ladies—women, and children—are unknown in these ages and make one's blood run cold."[48]

Soon afterward, Britain sent fifteen thousand troops into India to quell the rebellion and immediately took control of India from the East India Company. Victoria was pleased to add such a rich and exotic new land to the British Empire—the largest overseas empire any country has ever ruled. She was more pleased still when a new title was bestowed upon her—Empress of India.

Exploring Africa

Some of Victorian Britain's foreign policy was motivated by the same evangelical spirit that motivated many toward humanitarian efforts, such as bringing about an end to slavery or aiding the poorest people in England. During the 1840s a new generation of missionaries and explorers began to focus on Africa. Some early explorers and traders had visited parts of the African shoreline and had even set up outposts in places like Cape Town, South Africa—a stopping-off place for British

The Scramble for Africa

For centuries English slave traders had captured and sold people—primarily from Africa—as slaves. In 1833 Britain called a halt to slave trading, but that was not the end of British business interests in Africa. England and other European countries wanted to exploit the raw, mostly unexplored continent. The invention of iron-hulled ships with steam engines not only cut the travel time to India and the Far East, the steamers allowed easier exploration of the inlands of Africa. River maps were made, and friendly relationships were established with many of the tribal chiefs. This opened the doors to other travelers who were backed by wealthy business interests.

By the end of the century England and its European competitors had colonized nearly all of Africa, with the British possessing countries from Egypt in the north—where they built the Suez Canal—to Cape Town in the south, where they discovered gold and diamonds. Armed conflicts, such as the Boer Wars, were fought to establish control of areas that had such valuable resources. Other countries—Spain, Italy, Germany, France, Belgium, and Holland—were also drawn into the frenzy to colonize and monopolize areas of Africa. These countries were attracted by the ample supplies of copper, cotton, rubber, palm oil, cocoa, tea, gold, and tin, which were used for many items popular with Europeans.

ships journeying around Africa en route to India. But few had ventured inland, believing that there was little but desert or wasteland within the continent.

The most famous of the British explorers to travel to Africa was David Livingstone. A physician and missionary, Livingstone was motivated by his desire to abolish the slave trade that was still thriving in Africa. He also was eager to see for himself the wonders of the African interior. The first European to cross the Kalahari Desert in southern Africa, he was also the first European to see the world's largest waterfall, which is located on the Zambezi River in what is now the nation of Zambia. In his queen's honor Livingstone named it Victoria Falls.

Throughout his years in Africa Livingstone showed great respect for the native people he encountered. He died in 1873 after a long bout of dysentery and malaria. Two of his closest African friends prepared his body for the journey back to England but cut his heart out and buried it under a tree near the spot where he died—because they knew his heart belonged in Africa.

The Crimean War

One of the exceptions to Britain's policy of avoiding military conflict during the Victorian era was the Crimean War, which began in 1853, during the early part of Victoria's reign. It got its name from the Crimea, a peninsula on the northern coast of the Black Sea, which was part of the Turkish Empire. The war began when Russia invaded the Crimea, hoping to control the strait between Turkey and Europe.

Britain and France had long been concerned about the ambitions of Czar Nicholas I to expand his territory. Victoria and her ministers were especially worried that Britain's access to the Mediterranean trade routes would be cut off by the Russian action in the Crimea. For that reason Britain agreed to join the French and Turks in fighting the Russian army. France was also motivated by the opportunity to demonstrate a military show of force that had been lacking in its last battle at Waterloo.

Hardships arose almost from the beginning. Soon after arriving in Turkey, more than eight thousand soldiers were laid low by cholera and malaria. In addition to the spread of disease, the British army was compromised by disorganization. Britain had not fought in a major conflict since the Battle of Waterloo against Napoleon in 1815, and the Crimean War quickly brought into sharp focus how the military had regressed since that time.

Because of corruption and inefficiency in the Commissariat, the branch that supplied weapons, rations, and equipment to the military, the army was lacking in even the most basic supplies and equipment. For example, so few British soldiers had boots that it was commonplace for them to trade their precious food rations to French soldiers who had an extra pair. British supply ships were slow to arrive in the Crimea, and when they did, they contained none of the much-needed building supplies for the troops to erect medical shelters and barracks. And for some inexplicable reason, the Commissariat sent right and left boots in separate ships, so there were long delays in the soldiers getting their footwear.

Underqualified Officers

The disorganization was not confined to weapons and gear. The commanding officers of the British army lacked experience and training. For many years there had been a custom in Britain of allowing men of the aristocracy to purchase commissions, or high military ranks, for themselves and their sons. At the beginning of the war that custom, as well as the method of deciding rank based on seniority, was still in effect.

That meant that virtually all of the army's senior officers were older men who had fought in the Napoleonic Wars or wealthy, upper-crust men who had neither experience in nor knowledge of military matters. Notes historian Byron Farwell, "They might be stone-deaf, one-eyed, lacking an arm or a leg, and approaching senility—all but one of the Generals commanding the British forces in the Crimea were over 60, which was old, for those days—but as long as they were socially 'the right sort' they were welcomed."[49]

One example was Lord Raglan, who was made commander in chief of the British army in the Crimea. Historians say that Raglan was old and often confused during the war. "As a young man, he had fought in the Napoleonic Wars," notes Patrick N. Allitt, "and his memory of warfare was becoming very distant. In fact, [during the Crimean War] he always referred to the enemy as 'the French' . . . while in fact, France was one of Britain's allies."[50]

The Charge of the Light Brigade

The lowest point of the Crimean War—as well as the most infamous—was the result of muddled strategy and mixed signals. It occurred on October 25, 1854. The commanding officers were above the battlefield, watching the progress of the combat, when Lord Raglan sent a messenger to tell the Light Brigade of the British cavalry—more than six hundred saber-wielding soldiers mounted on light, fast horses—to pursue part of the Russian army as it moved some artillery. The message made no sense to the cavalry, since the only artillery they could see was in a valley surrounded on three sides by Russian troops. But because soldiers were never

Lord Raglan gives the order for the disastrous 1854 British cavalry charge immortalized in the poem "The Charge of the Light Brigade" by Alfred, Lord Tennyson. In this battle of the Crimean War, a large number of British soldiers were killed or wounded.

supposed to question the order of an officer, they mounted the charge.

The result was akin to mass suicide and predictably horrific. Of the approximately 600 members of the Light Brigade, a total of 387 officers and men, as well as 520 horses, were killed as they rode more than a mile into the valley toward the Russian guns. As there was no route out of the valley, those who survived had no choice but to turn around and ride back out the same way they rode in. One French officer, watching, cried, "Quel abattoir! [What a slaughterhouse!]"[51] A Russian cavalry officer was equally incredulous:

> It is difficult, if not impossible, to do justice to the feat of these mad cavalry, for, having lost a quarter of their number and being apparently impervious to new dangers and further losses, they quickly reformed their squadrons to return over the same ground littered with their dead and dying. With such desperate courage these valiant lunatics set off again, and not one of the living—even the wounded—surrendered.[52]

Though the men of the Light Brigade had conducted themselves bravely, it would be a mistake to view the charge as an important sacrifice in a major battle. Rather, it was an example of how poorly the British officers orchestrated their strategies and communicated with their soldiers. Says Crimean War historian Trevor Royle, "It was not just a heroic blunder. It was totally unnecessary."[53]

After the Crimean War, it was clear that Britain had no business fighting another war until the mistakes and inadequacies of its army were corrected. That, says historian Cecil Woodham-Smith, is the war's best legacy: "Even the incompetency of the Crimea bore fruit."[54]

Much of the Victorian era had been spent maintaining and adding to Britain's worldwide empire. However, by the latter years of Victoria's reign, many of those colonies were no longer satisfied with their status, and things would change.

Chapter 5

The Legacy of
Victorian England

O n January 22, 1901, Victoria died at age eighty-one. She had lived almost fifty years beyond the life expectancy for a woman born in 1819. She had been frail for years, suffering from fatigue, rheumatism, and poor eyesight. And while she had continued to appear at functions that demanded her presence, it had often been a struggle. She had been more withdrawn since Albert's death forty years before from typhoid fever and had continued to wear black mourning clothes until she died. But while not unexpected, the news of her death greatly saddened the people of Britain, most of whom had never experienced life under any other monarch.

In a letter to a friend, American-born writer Henry James, then living in England, expressed both his grief and his worry for the future of Britain without Victoria. "I mourn the safe and motherly old middle-class queen, who held the nation warm under the fold of her big, hideous Scotch plaid shawl, and whose duration had been so extraordinarily convenient and beneficent," he wrote. "I fear her death much more than I should have expected; she was a sustaining symbol."[55]

A Personal Legacy

Considering how long Victoria ruled, it is hardly surprising that she left an immense legacy. The Victorian years were rich in military and political events as well as cultural, literary, and scientific accomplishments.

But the most immediate and personal legacy was the transfer of power to her eldest son, Albert Edward. Known in his family as "Bertie," he chose the name Edward VII. He was nearly sixty when he ascended the throne and ruled for only nine years before he died in 1910.

Most of Victoria's other children married into various royal families throughout Europe. One of her grandsons, Wilhelm, was the son of her daughter Victoria, who married into German royalty. Ironically, Wilhelm eventually became Kaiser Wilhelm II, who went on to lead German forces against Britain during World War I. The current monarch of Britain, Elizabeth II, is the great-great-granddaughter of Queen Victoria.

A Different Sort of Empire

Historians point to the Victorian era as an important transition toward a more democratic Britain. During Victoria's reign, barriers that had prevented people from having their voices heard in Parliament were removed. Several reform acts increased the numbers of voters in Britain. For example, the Reform Act of 1867 extended voting privileges to an additional 1.5 million men—which doubled Britain's electorate among the middle and lower classes. After the Reform Act of 1884, suffrage had been extended to virtually the entire male working population. And although the issue of women's suffrage was gathering momentum, women did not get the vote until 1918, after World War I.

Since Victorian times, the British Empire has changed, too. For generations the English people were proud to say that "the sun never sets on the British Empire," for it was so vast that at any given time at least one of Britain's colonies would be experiencing daylight. But the colonies began peeling away in the later years of Victoria's reign. Canada had gained its independence in 1867; Australia did the same in 1901. In the years after Victoria's death, New Zealand and South Africa became independent, too. The bloody Indian Mutiny of 1857 set in motion a spirit of nationalism in India, which eventually gained its independence in 1947.

No Longer the Leader

Partly because of the erosion of its empire, Britain also lost its status as the manufacturing leader of the world. By the twentieth century both Germany and the United States had surpassed Britain. For many years

The Penny Black

Sending letters in the early part of Victoria's reign was often a nightmare. Senders had to go to the postmaster, who would hand stamp the letter with the date and time it was put in the mail. In those days postage could be collected from the person receiving the letter, and it was expensive. A letter carrier often had to make several calls on the recipient before he or she could amass the necessary funds to receive the letter. By 1835 the cost of receiving or sending a letter was so high that many could not afford the price—sometimes as much as a day's wages for working-class people.

In 1837, the year Victoria ascended the throne, a former English teacher named Rowland Hill proposed that all postage be prepaid, and to make the costs less, people could purchase adhesive-backed stamps for a penny each, which would cover the cost of mailing the letter. This system would also save time; there would be no need to stand in line at the post office to post a letter.

The first of these stamps was the Penny Black, issued in 1840. The gummed stamp was very small, with an image of Victoria on a black background, but because it was the first postage stamp in the world there was no need to add the country's name.

colonies such as Australia, Canada, and India had supplied British factories with cheap raw materials as well as ready markets for British finished products. With the loss of its colonies, British manufacturing suffered.

But historians say there were other causes for Britain's loss of manufacturing greatness. One was that many middle-class business owners refused to modernize their equipment, to put money back into businesses so they could grow and expand. Instead, many put their wealth into what really mattered in Britain—having prestige. Because status had been determined for centuries by family title and ownership of land, the newly wealthy were more interested in purchasing estates and expensive possessions that might allow them to find their way into higher society.

Another reason was that unlike Germany and the United States, Britain did not prepare students for careers that demanded innovation and advanced technical skills. Instead, parents wanted their children to become what generations of British parents had wanted for their children—to be respected politicians or church leaders. Notes historian Paul Johnson, "The English had a particular order of priorities in the way in which they invested their brain power, and industry certainly came low down the scale. The elite educational system was geared to produce above all, politicians, lawyers, and churchmen. It deliberately and systematically encouraged the ablest young men to aspire to be prime ministers, lord chancellors, and archbishops."[56]

The First War Correspondent

Some of the most lasting Victorian legacies originated in war—particularly the Crimean War. Though it was a disaster of military leadership and planning, some positive outcomes resulted from it. One was the advent of on-the-scene war reporting.

In the twenty-first century, television viewers take it for granted that there will always be news correspondents reporting from the sites of the big stories—from the Boston Marathon bombing of 2013 to an air strike in war-torn Syria. However, on-the-spot reporting of a foreign war was unheard of until February 1854, when William Howard Russell, a reporter for the London *Times*, was sent to the Crimea by his editor. This was an enormous novelty, for not until the telegraph was invented—and undersea cables laid—could a reporter on one continent file a story for a newspaper on another continent and have it printed in the next morning's edition. The cables connecting Britain with the rest of Europe—including Turkey—enabled Russell to do just that.

Russell's style was different from that of other writers, too. In times past, those who wrote battlefield memoirs tended to glorify wars rather than to describe the true experience of battle. Although Russell was clearly supportive of the fighting men, his reporting was also vivid and gritty. John Thadeus Delane, Russell's editor, explained later how his reporter was able to gain such detailed information for his dispatches: "Russell made friends with junior officers, and from them and other ranks, and by observation, gained his information. He wore quasi-military clothes and was armed, but did not fight. . . . His reports were vivid, dramatic, interesting, and convincing. . . . His reports identified with the British forces and praised British heroism. He exposed logistic and medical bungling and failure and the suffering of the troops."[57]

It was Russell who exposed the lack of supplies faced by the British soldiers, as well as their fifty-year-old dress uniforms that were more appropriate for formal occasions than for combat. In one of his dispatches, he describes how "[the regiments] came on solid and compact as blocks of marble, the sun dancing on their polished bayonets and scarlet coats. . . . All the men are as red in the face as turkeycocks—they seem to be gasping for breath . . . the coat is buttoned tightly up also to aid the work of suffocation and the belts and buckles compress the unhappy soldier where he most requires ease."[58]

But by far the most memorable of Russell's stories were those that detailed the filth and disease that were weakening the British troops day by day. He describes a makeshift hospital in which the most basic supplies were lacking. "There is not the least attention paid to decency or cleanliness—the stench is appalling—the fetid air can barely struggle out to taint the atmosphere, save through the chinks in the walls and roofs," he writes, "and, for all I can observe, these men die without the least effort being made to save them."[59]

Florence Nightingale

One of Russell's most avid readers during the early stages of the Crimean War was a young Englishwoman named Florence Nightingale. She had always wanted to become a nurse, but because she was part of a wealthy family, her parents discouraged it. Young women from wealthy families rarely worked, and those who did would never think of a service occupation like nursing, which was seen by many as little better than

Florence Nightingale talks with an army officer in a hospital ward in the Crimea. Nightingale organized and trained nurses to provide clean hospitals and quality care for injured soldiers. Her efforts ushered in the age of modern nursing.

prostitution. However, Nightingale eventually convinced them, and in October 1854 she set out for the Crimea, hoping to make a difference.

Even though she knew from Russell's reporting that there was a crisis in the medical treatment of the soldiers, she was unprepared for what she saw when she arrived in Scutari, Turkey. Wounded and dying men lay next to others in the throes of cholera, the stench of decay made it almost impossible to breathe, and maggots were everywhere. She writes:

> There were no vessels for water or utensils of any kind; no soap, towels, or clothes, no hospital clothes; the men lying in their

uniforms, stiff with gore and covered with filth to a degree and of a kind no one could write about; their persons covered with vermin. . . . We have not seen a drop of milk, and the bread is extremely sour. The butter is most filthy; it is Irish butter in a state of decomposition; and the meat is more like moist leather than food. Potatoes we are waiting for, until they arrive from France.[60]

Nightingale quickly organized a staff made up of fourteen trained nurses and twenty-four Catholic and Anglican nuns who set to scrubbing and cleaning the facilities. Nurses in those days were not highly trained but rather were hired to sit with ill or dying patients—either in charity hospitals or in the patients' own homes. They had no medical background, but, as Sally Mitchell notes, "because they stayed constantly with their patients they might be more perceptive than doctors in tracing the course of a disease and understanding the effects of certain treatments."[61]

Nightingale and her small, dedicated staff completely changed the image of nursing. Under her leadership nursing became a more respectable career, especially for young women. In her honor, people poured donations into a special fund at London's St. Thomas's Hospital to train nurses. Nursing was no longer limited to private homes or charity hospitals. Finally, since 1912 the International Red Cross has awarded the Florence Nightingale Medal every two years to nurses for outstanding service.

Social Issues and Literature

While many reforms occurred in the military and medicine as a result of the work of Russell and Nightingale, many of Britain's social ills were highlighted by novelists writing during the Victorian era. Without question, the most famous of these was Charles Dickens, whose books, including *Oliver Twist*, *Great Expectations*, and *A Christmas Carol*, are as popular in the twenty-first century as they were in Victorian England.

As a boy, Dickens worked ten-hour days at a blacking factory that made shoe polish for boots. His father had been imprisoned for debt, and Charles had to work to support himself. His experiences in the run-down old building, as well as the men who were his employers and the children who were his coworkers, were fodder for novels including *Oliver Twist* and *Hard Times*. He later told friend and biographer John Forster that the images from his youth remained with him:

> The blacking-warehouse was the last house on the left-hand side of the way, at old Hungerford Stairs. It was a crazy, tumble-down old house, abutting of course on the river, and literally overrun with rats. Its wainscoted rooms, and its rotten floors and staircase, and the old grey rats swarming down in the cellars, and the sound of their squeaking and scuffling coming up the stairs at all times, and the dirt and decay of the place, rise up visibly before me, as if I were there again.[62]

Pollution and Greed

As a writer, Dickens called attention to the deplorable working conditions in factories, as well as the noise, filth, and pollution that resulted from them. For example, in *Hard Times* he invented a location based on Manchester, which he called Coketown:

> It was a town of machinery and tall chimneys, out of which interminable serpents of smoke trailed themselves for ever and ever, and never got uncoiled. . . . It had a black canal in it, and a river that ran purple with ill-smelling dye, and vast piles of building full of windows where there was a rattling and a trembling all day long, and where the piston of the steam-engine worked monotonously up and down, like the head of an elephant in a state of melancholy madness.[63]

His most enduring work is a novella called *A Christmas Carol*, about a miserly man, Ebenezer Scrooge, who is visited on Christmas Eve by three ghosts who hope to improve his outlook on humanity. Dickens's depiction of Scrooge has been seen as a commentary on the

Bob Cratchit carries Tiny Tim on his shoulder in this illustration from A Christmas Carol *by Charles Dickens. In his many books, Dickens exposed the dark underbelly of English life during the Victorian era.*

wealthy of Victorian times, who tended to blame the poor for their own problems and who turned a deaf ear when asked to contribute to charities. For example, on Christmas Eve two men come to his office collecting for the poor. Scrooge refuses, insisting that the poor already have plenty of options:

"Are there no prisons?" asked Scrooge.

"Plenty of prisons," said the gentleman, laying down the pen again.

"And the Union workhouses?" demanded Scrooge. "Are they still in operation?"

"They are. Still," returned the gentleman, "I wish I could say they are not. . . ."

"Oh! I was afraid, from what you said at first, that something had occurred to stop them in their useful course," said Scrooge, "I'm very glad to hear it."[64]

Whether it is performed as a play or a movie or read in its original form, the story of Scrooge's transformation from a mean miser to someone with charity and goodwill in his heart is considered by many to be a key part of their Christmas celebrations. But besides Dickens's classic, there are other Christmas traditions for which the Victorians can take credit.

Victorian Christmas

At the beginning of the nineteenth century, though many in England went to church on Christmas, the holiday was far from what it is in the twenty-first century. Most people worked on Christmas Day, and schools had no Christmas holidays. Families usually enjoyed a special dinner on Christmas Day and lit candles or burned a Yule log in the fireplace. Interestingly, there were no Christmas presents—the holiday for exchanging presents was New Year's Day. But by the end of the Victorian era, Christmas had grown to be the biggest celebration of the year.

Although the Christmas tree had long been a tradition in Germany, the ceremonial decorating of the tree had not caught on anywhere else. In 1841 Albert decided to bring an evergreen tree into Windsor Castle for his and Victoria's first Christmas together. He had enjoyed Christmas trees growing up in Germany, and Victoria was delighted with the custom. A few years later a London newspaper published an illustration of Victoria, Albert, and their children gathered around their decorated Christmas tree. Because the British public was so taken with the young royal couple, it was not long before most aristocratic and middle-class homes adopted the Christmas tree tradition, too. Year by year, Victorian trees became more lavish and ornate, decorated with berries, candies, and gingerbread men as ornaments.

Public Bathrooms

Perhaps the most useful legacy of the Great Exhibition was the public bathroom. Never before had anyone conceived of the idea of supplying multiple "water closets"—as bathrooms were often called then—in a large public place. The idea belonged to George Jennings, a plumber from southeast England. He installed flushing toilets in special rooms at the Crystal Palace, where, for the entrance fee of one penny, gentlemen could have a clean seat (attendants washed the seat off after each user was finished), a towel, a comb, and a shoeshine. Later, Jennings provided facilities for ladies, too.

The bathrooms were a huge financial success. More than 827,000 visitors took advantage of them during the Great Exhibition. Afterward, when the Crystal Palace was dissembled and rebuilt in Sydenham, the toilets were eventually installed at the new location. After the initial stir over Jennings's invention, the phrase "spend a penny" was used for many years as a euphemism for "needing to use the bathroom."

The first Christmas cards were created after Britain revamped its postal system in 1840 so that postage was inexpensive—only a penny to send a letter anywhere in England. In 1843 an entrepreneur named Sir Henry Cole was too busy to send individual Christmas greetings to all of his friends and business colleagues. Instead, he hired an artist to design an illustration of a Christmas scene. Cole had the image made into cards that he signed and mailed. The idea caught on quickly; by 1880 Christmas-card production had become a lucrative industry in England, with 11.5 million produced that year. Even so, many parents, including Victoria and Albert, preferred that their children draw their own cards and mail them to friends and family members.

The Legacy of "The Great Hunger"

The starvation of more than 1 million people in Ireland, beginning in 1845, and millions more immigrating to North America, Britain, and Australia has had long-lasting effects. One was the bitterness and anger of the Irish toward the British for their inaction during the famine.

In his 1860 book *The Last Conquest of Ireland (Perhaps)* Irish journalist John Mitchel writes, "The Almighty indeed sent the potato blight, but the English created the Famine."[65] Not only did the English landowners fail to take care of their starving tenants, but Parliament took too long to repeal the Corn Laws that protected English farmers—which resulted in more starvation.

By the late 1850s an Irish group known as the Fenians demanded that Ireland be allowed to rule itself rather than be ruled by the British Parliament. The prime minister at the time, William Gladstone, believed it was possible to appease Ireland by allowing the country to have its own parliament separate from that of England. However, Parliament could not agree on Home Rule, as it was called, and the anger continued to simmer throughout Victoria's reign. Not until after World War I was a modified version of Home Rule passed, forming an independent Republic of Ireland in the south of Ireland, and six mainly Protestant counties, known as Northern Ireland, that are still part of the United Kingdom.

Visitors to the Great Exhibition of 1851 look through a textile display. The exhibition broadly illustrated the innovations and enduring legacy of England's Victorian era.

However, Northern Ireland remains an unresolved issue. From the late 1960s through the late 1990s the region experienced many outbreaks of violence—known as "The Troubles"—between Catholic and Protestant terrorist organizations. These resulted in more than thirty-five hundred deaths. As of 2013 there have been numerous peace negotiations and a halt to the violence. Yet no formalized resolution on how Northern Ireland should be governed, and by whom, has taken place.

The Great Exhibition Lives On

The Great Exhibition of 1851 had a number of far-reaching legacies as well. One was the growing realization that the products and ideas of hard working manufacturers, artists, and scientists deserved recognition. For too long, many believed, work was viewed only as a means of acquiring money. But work for work's sake, notes James Wilson in an 1851 article in the *Economist*, was finally receiving the recognition it deserved: "Labour is ceased to be looked down upon. . . . The Bees are more considered than the Butterflies of society; wealth is valued less as an exemption from toil, than as a call to effort."[66]

Although the exhibition was not called a "fair," historians agree that it was truly the first World's Fair. In fact, since the Great Exhibition scores of other nations have hosted their own international exhibitions. Some of these, such as the Seattle World's Fair in 1962, were modeled after the Great Exhibition, showcasing a wide range of international accomplishments. Others, like the World Horticultural Exhibition of 1999, held in Kumming, China, have been specific to a certain type of endeavor. The most recent World's Fair was held in Yeosu, South Korea, in 2012.

Victoria, the Icon

Victoria's name has been memorialized in cities, such as the capital of British Columbia, as well as the largest waterfall in the world. It was she who in 1856 initiated the Victoria Cross, a medal originally made from metal melted down from cannons captured from the Russians in the Crimean War. It remains today Britain's highest military decoration for bravery.

But her greatest legacy is the name of the era in which she ruled. During those years Britain was a land of stark contrasts and rapid change. The era saw economic and political struggles, heartbreaking social problems, the growth of the empire, a whirlwind of technological and scientific progress—and Victoria has become the symbol of it all.

Source Notes

Introduction: What Were the Defining Characteristics of Victorian England?
1. Quoted in Queen Victoria Online, "Queen Victoria's Coronation." www.queenvictoriaonline.com.
2. Quoted in EyeWitness to History, "Victoria Becomes Queen." www.eyewitnesstohistory.com.
3. Quoted in PBS, *Queen Victoria's Empire*, PBS Home Video, 2006.
4. Quoted in Library of America, "Queen Victoria's Jubilee." www.loa.org.
5. Edward Larsen, telephone interview by author, March 19, 2013.

Chapter One: What Conditions Led to the Victorian Era?
6. Quoted in PBS, *Queen Victoria's Empire*.
7. Quoted in Patrick N. Allitt, *Victorian Britain*, Part 1, course guidebook, Great Courses, 2002, p. 47.
8. Frances Ann Kemble, *Records of a Girlhood*. Middlesex, UK: Echo Library, 2008, pp. 239–40.
9. Quoted in EyeWitness to History, "The Execution of Louis XVI, 1793." www.eyewitnesstohistory.com.
10. Quoted in J.C.D. Clark, *Edmund Burke: Reflections on the Revolution in France*. Palo Alto, CA: Stanford University Press, 2001, p. 446.
11. Quoted in Walter E. Houghton, *The Victorian Frame of Mind, 1830–1870*. New Haven, CT: Yale University Press, 1957, p. 55.
12. Houghton, *The Victorian Frame of Mind*, pp. 54–55.
13. A.N. Wilson, *The Victorians*. New York: W.W. Norton, 2003, pp. 16–17.
14. Quoted in Simon Jenkins, *A Short History of England*. New York: Public Affairs, 2011, p. 242.
15. Jenkins, *A Short History of England*, p. 242.

16. Charles Petrie, *The Victorians*. London: Eyre & Spottiswoode, 1960, p. 40.
17. Quoted in PBS, *Queen Victoria's Empire*.

Chapter Two: The Working-Class Life

18. Quoted in Liza Picard, *Victorian London: The Tale of a City, 1840–1870*. New York: St. Martin's, 2006, p. 75.
19. Quoted in Wilson, *The Victorians*, p. 155.
20. Quoted in PBS, *Queen Victoria's Empire*.
21. The Victorian Web, "Child Labor." www.victorianweb.org.
22. Picard, *Victorian London*, p. 73.
23. Patrick N. Allitt, "Poverty and the 'Hungry Forties,'" in *Victorian Britain,* video recording, 2002.
24. Quoted in Wilson, *The Victorians*, p. 12.
25. Quoted in Christopher Hudson, "Workhouse of Horrors: How This Medieval Hell of Beatings and Sack Cloth Exists Within Living Memory," *Mail Online,* August 12, 2008. www.dailymail.co.uk.
26. Sally Mitchell, *Daily Life in Victorian England*. Westport, CT: Greenwood, 2009, p. 289.
27. Quoted in Daniel Pool, *What Jane Austen Ate and Charles Dickens Knew*. New York: Touchstone, p. 242.
28. Quoted in Sally Ledger and Holly Furneaux, eds., *Charles Dickens in Context*. Cambridge: Cambridge University Press, 2011.
29. Quoted in Heather Shore, *Artful Dodgers: Youth and Crime in Early Nineteenth Century London*. Rochester, NY: Royal Historical Society, Boydell, 1999, p. 130.
30. Richard D. Altick, *Victorian People and Ideas: A Companion for the Modern Reader of Victorian Literature*. New York: W.W. Norton, 1973, p. 95.

Chapter Three: Science and Technology in the Victorian Era

31. Quoted in Petrie, *The Victorians*, p. 164.
32. Quoted in Elizabeth Burton, *The Pageant of Early Victorian England*. New York: Charles Scribner's Sons, 1972, p. 14.
33. Roy Porter, *The Greatest Benefit to Mankind: A Medical History of Humanity*. New York: W.W. Norton, 1997, p. 403.

34. Quoted in Picard, *Victorian London*, p. 192.
35. Victor Robinson, *The Story of Medicine*. New York: New Home Library, 1943, pp. 420–21.
36. Picard, *Victorian London*, pp. 186–87.
37. Quoted in Cecil Woodham-Smith, *Queen Victoria: From Her Birth to the Death of the Prince Consort*. New York: Knopf, 1972, p. 328.
38. Quoted in Picard, *Victorian London*, p. 188.
39. Quoted in Thomas Hart, "Darwin and the Removal of Design," The Victorian Web. www.victorianweb.org.
40. Quoted in Patrick N. Allitt, "Progress and Optimism," in *Victorian Britain*, Part 2, video recording.
41. Allitt, "Progress and Optimism."
42. Quoted in Paul Thomas Murphy, *Shooting Victoria: Madness, Mayhem and the Rebirth of the British Monarchy*. New York: Pegasus, 2012, p. 344.

Chapter Four: Empire Building and Maintenance

43. John Kelly, *The Graves Are Walking: The Great Famine and the Saga of the Irish People*. New York: Henry Holt, 2012, p. 38.
44. Quoted in DoChara.com, "The Irish Potato Famine." www.dochara.com.
45. Quoted in Ireland: Between History and Memory, "Eyewitness Accounts of the Famine." http://blogs.evergreen.edu.
46. Quoted in Internet Archive, "Substance of the Speeches of William Wilberforce," number 54. www.archive.org.
47. Quoted in Mitchell, *Daily Life in Victorian England*. p. 275.
48. Quoted in Mia Carter and Barbara Harlow, eds., *Archives of Empire, vol. 1: From the East India Company to the Suez Canal*, Durham, NC: Duke University Press, 2003, p. 481.
49. Quoted in Picard, *Victorian London*, p. 111.
50. Patrick N. Allitt, "The Crimean War," in *Victorian Britain*, Part 2, video recording.
51. Quoted in Wilson, *The Victorians*, p. 183.
52. Quoted in Trevor Royle, *Crimea: The Great Crimean War, 1854–1856*. New York: St. Martin's, 2000, p. 274.
53. Royle, *Crimea*, p. 275.

54. Quoted in Cecil Woodham-Smith, *The Reason Why*. New York: McGraw-Hill, 1953, p. 271.

Chapter Five: The Legacy of Victorian England

55. Quoted in Wilson, *The Victorians*, p. 6.
56. Quoted in Patrick N. Allitt, "The Victorian Legacy," in *Victorian Britain*, Part 2, video recording.
57. Quoted in Spartacus Educational, "William Howard Russell." www.spartacus.schoolnet.co.uk.
58. Quoted in Elizabeth Grey, *The Noise of Drums and Trumpets: W.H. Russell Reports from the Crimea*. New York: Henry Z. Walck, 1971, p. 41.
59. Quoted in Grey, *The Noise of Drums and Trumpets*, p. 152.
60. Quoted in The Victorian Web, "Florence Nightingale." www.victorianweb.org.
61. Mitchell, *Daily Life in Victorian England*, p. 205.
62. Quoted in World History Project, "1824: Charles Dickens Begins Working at Warren's Blacking Factory." http://timelines.com.
63. Quoted in PBS, "Queen Victoria's Empire."
64. Charles Dickens, *A Christmas Carol*. New York: Holiday House, 1983, p. 9.
65. Quoted in Wilson, *The Victorians*, p. 80.
66. James Wilson, "The First Half of the Nineteenth Century: Progress of the Nation and the Race (1851)," The History Muse. http://historymuse.net.

Important People of the Victorian Era

Prince Albert: The husband of Queen Victoria. Born a prince in Saxe-Coberg-Gotha, Albert was a first cousin of Victoria. He was responsible for the idea and much of the planning of the Great Exhibition of 1851. He died of typhoid fever in December 1861, leaving nine children.

Isambard Kingdom Brunel: An inventor and engineer during the early Victorian era, Brunel built the first oceangoing steamships, greatly reducing the length of ocean voyages.

Charles Darwin: A naturalist and the author of *On the Origin of Species*, published in 1859, Darwin presented evidence that plants and animals had changed over millions of years to adapt to their environments. Though many scientists hailed the book as a breakthrough, many traditional Christians were outraged because it contradicted the Bible's version of Creation.

Charles Dickens: A novelist and social critic, Dickens's books highlight the dismal social and employment conditions of the city's poor as well as the inhumane treatment of people in the workhouses. His works, such as *Oliver Twist* and *A Christmas Carol,* remain popular today.

David Livingstone: An explorer and missionary who journeyed to Africa in hope of ending the slave trade there, Livingstone was the first European to see the largest waterfall in the world, which he named Victoria Falls.

Florence Nightingale: The founder of modern nursing. Reading reports of the horrible state of medical treatment for British soldiers during the Crimean War, she gathered volunteers and went to the front lines to tend the sick and wounded. Nightingale is credited with making nursing a respected vocational choice.

James Raglan: The commander of the British forces in the Crimean War, Raglan had served in the military during the Napoleonic Wars early in the nineteenth century. He was blamed for key errors during the Crimean War that resulted in the deaths of many soldiers, including the failed charge of the Light Brigade.

William Howard Russell: A British journalist who reported from the front lines of the Crimean War. Because of the advent of telegraphic cables that connected continents, Russell was able to send his stories to his newspaper, which could print them the following day. Russell was also credited for exposing the bureaucratic weaknesses of the British military that caused the deaths of so many soldiers.

John Snow: A London physician, Snow followed through on a hunch that cholera might be a waterborne disease rather than one spread by means of foul air. He also spent time as Victoria's doctor and administered chloroform to her when she delivered her eighth child.

James Watt: A Scottish inventor whose steam engine is credited with setting the Industrial Revolution in motion. Though he did not invent the steam engine, he adapted it so it was smaller and more efficient, enabling it to be used in locomotives, mills, and factories.

Victoria: The queen of Britain from 1837 to 1901, Victoria ruled longer than any monarch in British history. She was married to Prince Albert, and with him had nine children. Her reign is linked with Britain's greatest period of expansion and an unprecedented era of scientific and technological advance.

For Further Research

Books

DK/Smithsonian, *Modern History in Pictures: A Visual Guide to the Events That Shaped Our World*. New York: DK, 2012.

John Kelly, *The Graves Are Walking: The Great Famine and the Saga of the Irish People*. New York: Henry Holt, 2012.

Thomas Keneally, *Three Famines: Starvation and Politics*. New York: Serpentine, 2011.

Mike Manning and Brita Granstrom, *Charles Dickens: Scenes from an Extraordinary Life*. London: Frances Lincoln, 2011.

Sally Mitchell, *Daily Life in Victorian England*. Westport, CT: Greenwood, 2009.

Paul Thomas Murphy, *Shooting Victoria: Madness, Mayhem and the Rebirth of the British Monarchy*. New York: Pegasus, 2012.

Helen Rappaport, *A Magnificent Obsession: Victoria, Albert, and the Death That Changed the British Monarchy*. New York: St. Martin's, 2012.

William Howard Russell et al., *The Crimean War: As Seen by Those Who Reported It*. Edited by Angela Michelli Fleming and John Maxwell Hamilton. Baton Rouge: Louisiana State University Press, 2009.

Kate Williams, *Becoming Queen Victoria: The Tragic Death of Princess Charlotte and the Unexpected Rise of Britain's Greatest Monarch*. New York: Ballantine, 2010.

Websites

Child Labour in Britain (www.spartacus.schoolnet.co.uk/IRchild.htm). This site contains a well-organized index of articles about the details of child labor in Britain that examines key people, categories of work children did, and details of reforms addressing the issue.

Crimean War Research Society (http://cwrs.russianwar.co.uk/cwrsentry.html). Included here are details on almost every aspect of the Crimean War, from key battles to songs written during the war. There is also a good section showing photographs of the sites of the major battles.

David Perdue's Charles Dickens Page (http://charlesdickenspage.com). This site contains everything—from a map of Dickens's London and details about the writing of his books to an exhaustive glossary explaining words and references in his books that might confound a modern reader.

History Place: Irish Potato Famine (www.historyplace.com/worldhistory/famine). A good website that includes a helpful bibliography and interesting articles on various aspects of the famine, such as its causes, coffin ships and emigration, and the role of the English in the disaster.

Indian Mutiny, 1857–58 (www.britishempire.co.uk/forces/armycampaigns/indiancampaigns/mutiny/mutiny.htm). A complete site with excellent explanation of the causes and background of the uprising and a good timeline of the conflict. Especially interesting are a series of colorful maps of the region from 1857.

Queen Victoria's Scrapbook (www.queen-victorias-scrapbook.org/index.html). This website allows users to view some of Queen Victoria's thousands of journal entries as well as to hear audio, see photos, and actually view the journals of selected occasions in the queen's life in her own handwriting.

Victorian Britain: History Trails (www.bbc.co.uk/history/trail/victorian_britain/social_conditions/victorian_urban_planning_01.shtml). A wealth of information, from the role of women in Victorian England to the role of political cartoons in the nineteenth century. Also included are learning games and quizzes for children and adults.

The Victorian Literary Studies Archive (http://lang.nagoyau.ac.jp/~matsuoka/Victorian.html). A helpful site with links to excellent information and colorful illustrations of Victorian-era children's literature, costumes of the day, and a fascinating link to letters written by a Victorian governess during a trip to India.

The Victorian Web (www.victorianweb.org). A comprehensive website that includes information about authors, scientists, politicians, artists, and dozens of other categories of people, as well as more than sixty-one thousand images and documents relevant to Victorian England. Also a good source for primary sources related to events that occurred during the Victorian era.

Index

Picture Credits

About the Author

Gail Stewart is the author of more than two hundred books for children, teens, and young adults. She lives in Minneapolis with her husband, Carl, and is the mother of three grown sons: Theo, Elliot, and Flynn.